JOURNEYS

Units 1–5

READING
Adventures

Unit 6

Make
Your Mark

HOUGHTON MIFFLIN HARCOURT
School Publishers

From *Judy Moody* by Megan McDonald, illustrated by Peter H. Reynolds. Text Copyright © 2000 by Megan McDonald, illustrations copyright © 2000 by Peter H. Reynolds. Reprinted by permission of Candlewick Press, Santillana Publishing Company, Inc. and the author. "Fast Track" by Nikki Grimes. Copyright © 1999 by Nikki Grimes. Reprinted by permission of Curtis Brown Ltd. "Ode to My Shoes" from *From the Bellybutton of the Moon and Other Summer Poems/ Del ombligo de la luna y otras poemas de verano*. Copyright © 1998 by Francisco X. Alarcón. Reprinted by permission of the publisher, Children's Book Press, San Francisco, CA, www.childrensbookpress.org. "Magnet" from *All The Small Poems and Fourteen More* by Valerie Worth. Text copyright © 1994 by Valerie Worth. Reprinted by permission of Farrar, Straus and Giroux LLC. "Science Fair Project" from *Almost Late to School and More School Poems* by Carol Diggory Shields. Text copyright © 2003 by Carol Diggory Shields. All rights reserved including the right of reproduction in whole or in part in any form. Reprinted by permission of Dutton Books, a member of Penguin Young Readers Group, a division of Penguin Group (USA) Inc., and Carol Diggory Shields. "I chop chop chop without a stop..." from *Good Sports* by Jack Prelutsky. Text copyright © 2007 by Jack Prelutsky. Reprinted by permission of Alfred A. Knopf, an imprint of Random House Children's Books, a division of Random House, Inc. "Long Jump" from *Swimming Upstream: Middle School Poems* by Kristine O'Connell George. Text copyright © 2002 by Kristine O'Connell George. Reprinted by permission of Houghton Mifflin Harcourt Publishing Company and the author. "Defender" from *Tap Dancing on the Roof: Sijo (Poems)* by Linda Sue Park. Text copyright © 2007 by Linda Sue Park. Reprinted by permission of Houghton Mifflin Harcourt Publishing Company and Curtis Brown Ltd. "Spellbound" from *The Dog Ate My Homework* by Sara Holbrook. Text copyright © 1996 by Sara Holbrook. Reprinted by permission of Boyds Mills Press, Inc. "Company's Coming" from *The Alligator in the Closet and Other Poems Around the House* by David L. Harrison. Text copyright © 2003 by David L. Harrison. Reprinted by permission of Wordsong, a division of Boyds Mills Press Inc.

Copyright © 2012 by Houghton Mifflin Harcourt Publishing Company

Printed in the U.S.A.

ISBN: 978-0-547-59583-2

5 6 7 8 9 10 0868 20 19 18 17 16 15 14 13 12 11

4500304940   B C D E F G

READING Adventures

The ROBODOGS of Greenville

by Thomas S. Park   illustrated by John Hovell

Characters

Narrator	Cosmo	Professor
Diz	Robodog	Captain Spacely

SCENE 1
Setting: Diz's house

Narrator: This story takes place in the year 2222 in a small town called Greenville. Greenville is a friendly little community, just like many other towns. Everyone gets along there.

Diz: Hi, Cosmo! Thanks for coming over.

Cosmo: Anytime, Diz! How are things over at your dad's hydro car store?

Diz: Really busy, Cosmo.

Cosmo: I hear they're selling those hydro cars faster than the factory on planet Mars can make them!

Narrator: Diz and Cosmo live with their families in Greenville. Their parents fly the children to school in the family hydro cars. The children chat with their friends each evening on the family televideocomputers. They also play with their family dogs.

Diz: Here, Robodog! Catch the flying disk!

Robodog: I am coming, Owner Diz. I will catch the disk.

Narrator: There is one unusual thing about the dogs in Greenville. All the dogs are robots.

Diz: Good catch, Robodog.

Robodog: Thank you, Owner Diz. What can I do for you now?

Narrator: The robodog is the only kind of dog in Greenville. Scientists have built robodogs to be better than real dogs. They can speak. They can take care of chores such as cleaning and cooking. They can even beam movies from their eyes onto a wall.

Cosmo: Last night, our robodog showed us an old movie.

Diz: What was it about?

Cosmo: It was about a real dog. She was beautiful!

Diz: A real dog? What was she like?

Cosmo: A lot like our robodogs. She could do tricks and help her owners.

Diz: Could she speak?

Cosmo: She could only make a sound called barking. She didn't know any human words.

Diz: Really? That's strange.

Robodog: Yes. That is very strange, Owner Diz.

Cosmo: Robodog, I'm hungry. Would you go to the kitchen and make sandwiches for Diz and me, please?

Robodog: I will be right back, Owner Diz and Friend Cosmo.

Cosmo: The dog in the movie seemed to love her owner. She was sweet and cuddly. She didn't just work around the house.

Diz: The dog loved her owner? I wish my robodog were like that.

Narrator: You see, robodogs are helpful and can do tricks, but they are not sweet or cuddly.

Cosmo: Maybe we should talk to the professor about this.

SCENE 2
Setting: The professor's house

Narrator: The professor is an expert on animals. So Diz and Cosmo go to talk to the professor about the differences between real dogs and robodogs.

Professor: Yes, Diz and Cosmo. It's true that real dogs could be happy or sad. They could even show love.

Diz: Why don't our robodogs show emotion?

Dog — Happy — Sad

Robodog — No Emotic

Professor: Scientists don't know how to make dogs that act like friends. They can make them useful, but not loving.

Cosmo: My robodog cleans my room, makes my meals, and helps me with my homework.

Diz: Robodogs aren't very cuddly!

Cosmo: I know. After Robodog has done its chores or tricks, it just switches off.

Professor: That's right. It dozes. The scientists made robodogs that way to save energy.

Diz: I wish I had a real dog.

Cosmo: There aren't any more real dogs. They disappeared permanently from Earth a hundred years ago.

Professor: It's funny that you should say that. I just got off my Intergalactic Computer Phone with the famous explorer Captain Spacely. He told me about an astonishing discovery. Maybe he can tell you about it, too. Computer Phone, call Captain Spacely.

Spacely: Captain Spacely here. Professor, do you want to hear more about my discovery?

Professor: Yes, indeed I do, Captain. Tell my friends Diz and Cosmo what you have found.

Spacely: I can do better than that. I'll show them what I've found!

Narrator: Captain Spacely steps away from the computer phone. Diz and Cosmo hear a whining sound. Then they hear barking.

Diz: What is that strange sound?

Cosmo: I heard that sound in the movie. It's the barking sound a real dog makes!

Narrator: Captain Spacely is visible on the screen again. He beckons to a furry thing that leaps into his arms. Cosmo and Diz see that it looks something like a robodog, but it acts differently.

Spacely: I've found real dogs! There is a small planet that has many of the same animals that were once on Earth. In fact, it has so many kinds of animals that food and space are becoming hard to find.

Narrator: The dog in Captain Spacely's arms wags its tail and licks his face. Diz and Cosmo look at the dog with amazement.

Diz: I wish I could have one of those dogs!

Cosmo: Me, too!

Professor: I think that can be arranged. Tell them your plan, Captain Spacely!

Spacely: To help the animals, I am bringing a spaceship full of dogs back to Earth! There is lots of room on Earth for dogs. Cosmo and Diz, if you promise to care for them, you can have the first two!

Diz and Cosmo: Thanks, Captain Spacely!

> **SCENE 3**
> **Setting:** Diz's house

Narrator: Sure enough, Captain Spacely brings real dogs back to Earth. Cosmo and Diz get the first two dogs.

Diz: Give me a hug, Scooter!

Cosmo: Here, Rascal! Come and play with me!

Narrator: As for the robodogs, Cosmo and Diz decide to keep them. They come in handy when it is time to give Scooter and Rascal a bath.

Robodog: Owner Cosmo, should I get Rascal's bath ready?

Cosmo: Yes, Robodog. After that, would you take Rascal out for a walk?

Tell Me When

Tell Me Where

When you tell about something that happened, it is important to use words that tell **when** events happened. Time-order words such as *before*, *after,* and *then* help your listener understand the order of events.

> *After Robodog has done its chores or tricks, it just switches off.*

What word in this sentence helps you understand when Robodog switches off?

To give your listeners a clear picture, you also need to include words that tell **where** things are or where they happened.

> *Would you go to the kitchen and make sandwiches for Diz and me, please?*

What words in the sentence tell you where Robodog goes?

With a partner, take turns telling about an event in *The Robodogs of Greenville,* using words that tell *when* and *where.*

Have Your Say

Think about an experience you have had with an animal. It could be a pet or even an unusual zoo animal. Describe to your classmates what the animal was like and how you felt. Were you excited or afraid?

Before you talk about your experience, you will need to:
- think about details and words that describe how you felt.

As you are speaking, remember to:
- speak clearly in complete sentences.

As you are listening to one another speak, remember to:
- listen carefully so that you can ask questions when the speaker has finished.

When you are finished speaking, your classmates will ask you questions.

Your Turn
First, Next, Last

Good writers use time-order words and phrases such as *before, after, then,* and *last week* to help their readers understand the order of events in their writing.

In *The Robodogs of Greenville,* Cosmo and Diz are surprised that Captain Spacely discovered real dogs on another planet. Later, they are even more surprised when they receive the first two real dogs. The letter below is about another surprise. How do the time-order words and phrases in the letter help you understand the order of events?

Dear Justin,

You won't believe what happened to me last week! My mom left me clues for a treasure hunt. First, I had to go to the living room. Next, I had to go to the kitchen. Finally, I had to go to the basement. After a few seconds, I heard a funny sound. I walked toward the sound, where I found a new kitten waiting for me. I named the kitten Mia. I hope you will be able to meet her soon.

Sincerely,
Kayla

Reflect on Your Writing

Choose a friendly letter or a personal narrative that you have completed in class. As you read your writing, ask yourself these questions.

✓ Is it easy to understand the order of events in my writing?

✓ Where should I add words that tell about time order such as *before*, *after*, *then*, or *last week*?

✓ Where can I combine choppy sentences and make them compound sentences?

Answer the questions, and then edit your writing.

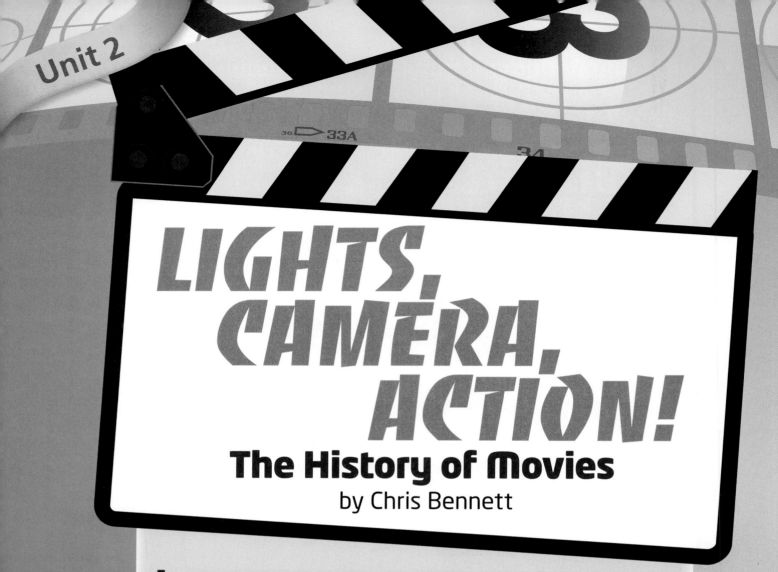

LIGHTS, CAMERA, ACTION!

The History of Movies

by Chris Bennett

Lights, camera, action! When you hear those words you think of movies. Just over one hundred years ago, movies were very different than they are today.

The first motion pictures in the late 1800s were moving pictures with no sound. They were only about a minute long. The early inventors worked hard to make moving pictures better. They designed new cameras to take pictures and record them on film, and projectors to show the pictures. Their designs and ideas led to today's movies, which are the most exciting and amazing movies ever!

Thomas Edison

Edison's Kinetoscope

The very first step toward making movies was the invention of photography in the 1820s. Photography is the process of making pictures with a camera. After this, inventors in the United States and other countries wanted a way to show motion, or the act of moving. The race was on!

One of the first people to succeed was an American, Thomas Edison. In 1889, he and his assistant, William Dickson, invented the kinetoscope. The kinetoscope used a camera, film, and an electric lamp.

Inside a four-foot high wooden box, a loop of film ran through a special camera. An electric lamp under the film lit images on the film as it passed through the camera. Our eyes see the quick movement of the images as motion. A peephole at the top of the box allowed a single person to view the moving pictures. At a kinetoscope parlor, the public watched motion pictures for the very first time.

In the 1890s, kinetoscope parlors opened all across the United States. At a parlor, a customer could view a different film in five different kinetoscopes for five cents each.

The Lumières' Motion-Picture Projector

Auguste and Louis Lumière

In Paris, Charles Antoine Lumière saw a movie through Edison's kinetoscope. He was impressed, but he believed his sons could design a better way to watch movies. His sons, Auguste and Louis, were two of the smartest scientists in Paris. They noticed one big problem with Edison's kinetoscope. Only one person could view the film at a time.

The Lumière brothers invented a camera and a projector that was one machine. They called their invention a *cinematographe*. The *cinematographe* recorded images on film which could be projected onto a screen. Many people could now sit together and watch larger moving images. The Lumières showed their movies to the public much like movie theaters do today.

This new entertainment was different and exciting. Nothing like it had ever been seen before!

The Lumière brothers presented their first motion picture show in December, 1895. Soon, they were showing their motion pictures in cities all over the world.

Nickelodeon storefront theater from the early 1900s

Early Movies and Movie Theaters

Soon, smaller, lighter movie projectors were being made in the United States. Movies became part of fairgrounds and "traveling tent" shows all over the country. The moving pictures had no sound, so narrators and musicians often traveled with the shows. They told the story and added music and sound effects to the moving pictures.

In 1902, *A Trip to the Moon* was one of the first movies that told a story.

The first movie theaters in the U.S were called *nickelodeons.* These small theaters charged a nickel to watch a movie. Movies, called *shorts*, were only about 15 minutes long. In a nickelodeon, a piano player often played along to the film as the audience watched.

What Next? Sound!

Even though there was no sound in early films, movies became more and more popular. In silent films, an actor's words were printed on the film and projected onto the screen, like words on a page.

The next challenge was to have sound to go with the images on the screen. People wanted to hear movies as well as see them. Moviemakers had always been interested in sound. The invention of a new kind of film in 1919 made sound on film possible. A camera was able to record images and sound on film at the same time. At first, the quality of the sound was poor. After many experiments, the quality improved. Big movie theaters started buying expensive sound systems. The public was very excited to hear what the actors were saying.

The new movies with sound were called *talkies.* The first full-length talkie was *The Jazz Singer* in 1927. The movie had both music and speaking. It was a smash success! Movies would never be silent again.

The Jazz Singer was the first feature film with dialogue and music.

The Wizard of Oz had lots of color!

Color Films

Another big step in the history of movies was adding color to film. Just as with sound, making movies with a lot of color took some time to get right. In some very early movies, color was painted onto film, frame by frame. Imagine a hand-painted film! Another method was to tint film by dipping it into a dye.

By the 1930s, a better process was used to make color movies. It used three layers of special color film. Each layer of film was a separate color. Together, they made all the colors.

One of the first color movies using the new process was *The Wizard of Oz* in 1939. This movie still looks great! Later, less expensive color film and cameras were designed.

Special Effects

For most of their history, movies have had special effects. These are tricks that make things seem different than they really are. Moviemakers can do amazing things with special effects.

Blue screen photography is a common special effect. Using blue screens, an actor can seem to be at the top of the Empire State Building, or flying over the Grand Canyon. The trick is that the actor never leaves the movie studio!

How does it happen? First, the actor is filmed in front of a blue screen. Next, a film of a background, such as the Grand Canyon, is made. Then the two pieces of film are put together to look like one very real scene.

Another special effect is called *slow motion.* A slow motion camera films action at a faster camera speed than normal. When a projector plays the film at normal speed, the action appears to slow down.

This actor is posing in front of a blue screen.

Today, most movie special effects are done using high-tech video cameras and computers. The process is called *CGI*, which means "computer-generated imagery." In 1993 *Jurassic Park* brought dinosaurs to life in a way that wowed audiences. Later, *Avatar* showed life on an imaginary planet in new ways. These movies could never have been made at an earlier time. In fact, the whole movie experience has changed a lot in just the last twenty years.

Now you can watch a 3-D movie in a special large theater with surround sound. Your seat moves back to view the action on a dome screen 72 feet high! In some theaters, you can even have dinner served with your movie.

Movies have come a long way since the silent movie shorts of the nickelodeon. Today's movies are much more thrilling than the first silent movies.

The movie *King Kong* was made in 1933. It had great special effects for a movie of its time, and it was a big hit with adult audiences. Sixty years later, *Jurassic Park* thrilled moviegoers with life-like dinosaurs.

Media Maze

When your parents went to school and wanted to find information on a topic, they may have read books, newspapers, and magazines. Today there are many other ways to find information.

Suppose you wanted to research movie special effects. You could still use books, magazines, or newspapers. You could also use many different kinds of media for your research. You could:

- search the Internet for websites about special effects.

- watch a video clip of a makeup artist working with an actor.

- study charts and graphs that give information about numbers or dates related to special effects.

- watch a TV show about the history of special effects.

As you explore different types of media, look for the main ideas and details in the information you find. This will help you understand and organize the information.

Media Presentations

1 Work with a partner or a small group. Choose and research a topic related to movies, such as silent movies, special effects, or cartoons.

2 Choose a type of media mentioned on the previous page to find information on your topic.

3 Note the main ideas and details in the material you select.

4 Present your findings to the class. Be sure to explain clearly the main ideas and details in your presentation.

5 Include a picture, a chart, a graph, or a short video clip to help support your presentation.

File   Edit   View   Favorites   Tools   Help

Search

Special Effects in the Movies

What's New   Trade Shows   Artist Spotlight   Awards

The latest monster movie is coming out with all the latest effects.

The Right Words Matter

CONNECTING WORDS

Good writers make their ideas clear to their readers. They use connecting words and phrases, such as *because*, *since*, and *for example*, to link their opinion and reasons.

What is the writer's opinion in the sentence below? What is the connecting word?

Special effects are astonishing because they make your imagination come alive.

WORDS AND PHRASES FOR EFFECT

Good writers also choose words and phrases that will cause their audience to feel a certain way.

What word does the author use for effect in the sentence below?

3-D movies are incredible.

Reflect on Your Writing

Choose the response to literature you wrote in this unit or another response piece. Look over your writing. Ask yourself these questions:

- Did I use connecting words to link my opinion and the reasons for my opinion?

- Where can I state my opinions and reasons more clearly?

- Where can I add words or phrases for effect?

Answer the questions and then edit your response.

Technology Wins the Game

by Mark Andrews

Almost everyone loves a good game. However, it's not just athletic ability or skill that helps sports players win. Many other things can contribute to a winning team or player. One of those things is the use of technology. Technology has made our lives easier and better in many ways. In sports, technology can help all types of athletes perform better.

It's All in the Design

If you like sports and science, being a sports engineer might be the job for you. Sports engineers are scientists who make sports more fun to play and to watch. They design better materials, surfaces, and equipment. They help keep athletes safe from injury. A sports engineer has probably helped to improve your favorite sport!

The Science of Sports Engineering

Some sports engineers study the way athletes move when they play different sports. An engineer might watch a soccer player to see how the player's foot strikes the ball. This can lead to ideas about soccer shoes, the soccer ball, or even the soccer field. Engineers use these ideas to improve the game in some way.

The first step for a sports engineer is to identify a problem in a sport—something to be improved. Almost anything can be improved! Then the sports engineer comes up with a possible solution. Next, he or she creates a model. The model may include a new kind of material. The new idea is then tested in a laboratory to see how well it works. Finally, the new product is tested by athletes. If it works well, soon athletes around the world will start to use it.

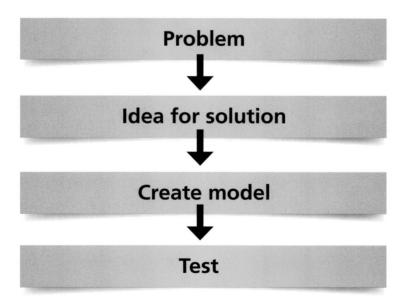

Problem

↓

Idea for solution

↓

Create model

↓

Test

Changing the Game

Let's take a look at tennis. This is a sport where sports engineers have made several changes.

What a Racket!

Tennis rackets have changed a lot. When the sport began, tennis rackets were made out of wood. Then in the 1960s, a metal racket was developed. Metal rackets were stronger and lighter than wood. Today, rackets are made out of different materials mixed together. These rackets are very light and provide more power than the old ones. The ball moves faster than ever.

Today's rackets also have a larger head, or string area, than before. This makes it easier for the tennis player to reach more balls. A player can also control the ball better and make it move in different ways.

More Bounce to the Ball

Tennis balls have come a long way, too. The first tennis balls were made of leather or cloth stuffed with wool or horsehair. These balls did not bounce very high. In the 1870s, rubber was first used to make tennis balls. These balls bounced better, but the cloth that covered the ball would fall off.

Today, tennis balls are still made of rubber. First, two matching "half-shell" pieces of rubber are joined together. This makes the hollow, round shape of the ball. Second, two pieces of felt are wrapped around the ball. Third, a rubber seam is added to keep the felt cover together. Finally, the balls are put in a can that is under pressure. This helps keep them bouncy. The whole process ensures that each tennis ball bounces the exact same way. Where the ball bounces is up to the player!

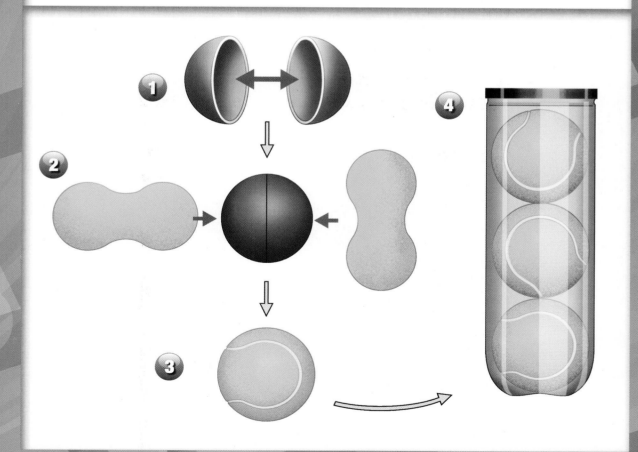

Higher and Faster

Sports engineers help athletes perform in just about every sport. Track and field athletes run, jump, and throw. Sports engineers help these athletes run faster, jump higher, and throw farther. They design new and better track and field equipment, surfaces, and clothing.

Jump Higher

Have you ever watched a pole vaulter at the Olympics? A good pole vaulter must have speed, strength, and the right pole. The pole must be flexible and strong enough to bend and lift the vaulter over the bar. Poles used to be made of wood. These were very stiff and heavy. Later, poles were made of more flexible bamboo. Then engineers designed poles made of aluminum. Today, poles are made of fiberglass and are very light. They bend easily. The more the pole bends, the further the vaulter sails through the air.

Run Faster

What makes a runner fast? Athletic ability and good training are most important. Engineers have designed new track surfaces and clothing to help.

Track runners used to run on grass fields. When it rained, the tracks would become soggy and slippery. Now, most runners run on "all-weather" tracks. These are man-made surfaces with a top coating of rubber chips. The rubber chips make the runners' shoes bounce off the track better. This increases speed.

New kinds of clothing also help runners speed up. Track stars don't wear shirts and shorts like they used to. They wear light-weight body suits that fit tightly. When they run in these suits, the wind does not slow them down. Every fraction of a second counts!

A New Kind of Racing

The Boston Marathon is the oldest and most famous marathon race in the world. Each year thousands of athletes run the 26-mile course through the hilly streets of Boston.

In 1975, Bob Hall finished the marathon in a different way. He wheeled his way to the finish line. Bob Hall was the first official wheelchair athlete to complete the Boston Marathon. He finished the race in less than 3 hours, faster than most runners.

▲ Bob Hall used a simple wheelchair in the Boston Marathon.

Today, wheelchair athletes compete with high-tech wheelchairs. ▶

In *These* Shoes?

Sport engineers have also designed athletes' shoes to make them faster and quicker and to give them more support. Athletes need different kinds of shoes for different sports. If you want to win, you need the right shoes!

A History of Running Shoes

In ancient times, runners ran barefoot. As time went on, athletes began to run in sandals. Soon, the sandal wearers were winning most of the races. The running shoe was born.

The next big change came in the 1800s in England. The first running shoe with a rubber sole was introduced. Rubber soles were light and comfortable. They also gripped the ground easily.

In the 1920s, a German named Adi Dassler sold the first modern running shoes with spikes. Spikes grip the ground and increase running speed.

Today, shoemakers and engineers better understand the science of running. Running shoes are made for every style of runner and any surface. Engineers know that runners need shoes that are strong and flexible.

Changes in Running Shoes

5th century B.C.
Ancient Greece: bare feet and sandals

1800s
shoes with rubber soles for a better grip

1920s
modern spiked running shoes

1979
air bubbles in sole for cushioning

2010
foam, silicone, air, gel cushioned shoes

Extra Bounce

Long jumpers need shoes that give the athletes extra bounce. The soles must be firm, but able to bend. These shoes have metal spikes in the front of the shoe only. This helps the jumper grip the ground and spring from the toes right before the jump.

Quick Movement

Soccer shoes have plastic or metal cleats, or rounded spikes, on the bottom. Cleats keep soccer players from slipping in the dirt, grass, and mud. Soccer players need to change directions quickly. Without cleats, soccer would be a slower, sloppier game!

Play Safely

Athletes also need special equipment and clothing to protect them from injury. Sports can be dangerous, and professional athletes often take risks.

Football Helmets

Over 100 years ago, football players did not wear helmets. Ouch! Then in the 1900s, players began to wear leather helmets. These early helmets did not provide much comfort or protection. Changes were needed. First, more padding was added. Second, a face mask was added to protect the nose and teeth. Also, the top of the helmet was made more round. This allowed a blow to slide off the helmet rather than strike head-on. Next, in 1939, the first plastic helmet was invented.

Today's football helmets are made of a special plastic that is light and strong. The helmet design protects players from head injuries. Some football helmets have tiny computer chips inside them. If a player hits his head, the chip sends a message to a computer on the sideline. The message helps doctors and coaches know if the player needs help.

Other Safety Features

Some ski clothes are made to help skiers in trouble. Sometimes back country skiers get lost or are injured miles away from anyone. Sports engineers developed special sensors for their clothing. The sensors send information about a skier's location. A rescue team receives the information. Then, they can find skiers who have fallen or are buried under the snow.

Brightly colored jackets and vests, called reflective wear, make bicyclists easier to see in the dark.

🔵 Just for Fun

The next time you play your favorite sport, think about some of the equipment you use. Think about the kind of surface you are standing, running, or jumping on. Notice how your sports shoes look or feel or help you perform. Now that you have read about sports engineering, you will probably think about how technology has helped to improve your sport. Technology not only makes our lives easier and better, but it also makes our lives a lot more fun!

Pleased, Happy, or Thrilled?

Some words, such as *pleased*, *happy*, and *thrilled*, have similar meanings. If you think about it, they are not exactly the same. When have you been pleased? happy? thrilled? Good writers and speakers choose words carefully so their audience will understand exactly what they mean. Read the words under the line. Which word sounds the least certain? the most certain?

thought — **wondered** — **believed** — **knew**

Read the sentences below. What is the meaning of each underlined word?

I <u>wondered</u> why you wanted to buy those shoes.

I just <u>knew</u> these new running shoes were going to help me run fast.

I <u>thought</u> your old shoes might be a problem.

Rewrite the sentences below, filling in the blanks with words from the word bank. Then share your sentences with a partner. Ask your partner what word he or she chose for each sentence.

thrilled
happy
pleased
content
sorry
gloomy
sad
unhappy

I am _____ track and field day is almost over.

Do you feel _____ about the 50-yard dash?

I am _____ with how I did.

Bring it to Life!

Good writers use clear, descriptive language to tell about the thoughts, feelings, and actions of people in a story. They use descriptive words and details to make the events and experiences come alive for their audience! As you read the paragraph below, notice the descriptive details. How does the writer describe the ball going over the goal? How does the writer feel about the game?

I waited eagerly all week for the soccer game to begin. The teams raced down the field. My teammates and I quickly chased the ball. I cornered the ball as I sprinted down the field. I swerved suddenly to my right and shifted my foot behind the ball. I kicked it straight at the net. The ball sailed high over the goal. I swirled around, disappointed, and jogged back to my team, ready to try again.

Reflect on Your Writing

Look back at the autobiography you wrote in Unit 3. Ask yourself these questions:

- Did I use words that clearly describe each character's actions?
- Did I use words that make the experience and events come alive to the reader?
- Did I use complete sentences?

If you answer **No** to any of the questions, edit your autobiography.

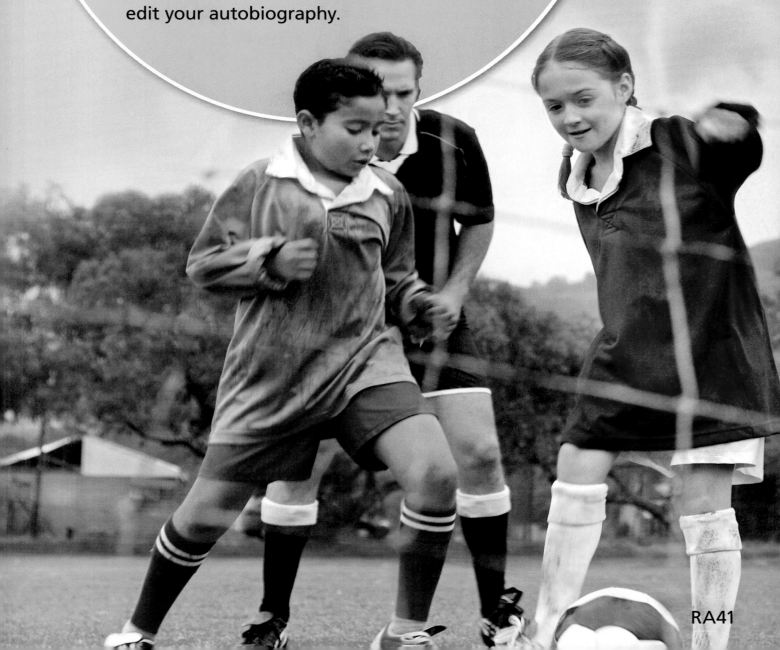

My Favorite Pet
My Smelly Pet

from Judy Moody

by Megan McDonald

illustrated by Peter H. Reynolds

My Favorite Pet

It was Labor Day, a no-school day. Judy looked up from her Me collage on the dining room table.

"We need a new pet," Judy announced to her family.

"A new pet? What's wrong with Mouse?" asked Mom. Mouse opened one eye.

"I have to pick MY FAVORITE PET. How can I pick my favorite when I only have one?"

"Pick Mouse," said Mom.

"Mouse is so old, and she's afraid of everything. Mouse is a lump that purrs."

"You're NOT thinking of a dog, I hope," said Dad. Mouse jumped off the chair and stretched.

"Mouse would definitely not like that," said Judy.

"How about a goldfish?" asked Stink. Mouse rubbed up against Judy's leg.

"Mouse would like that too much," Judy said. "I was thinking of a two-toed sloth."

"Right," said Stink.

"They're neat," said Judy. She showed Stink its picture in her rain forest magazine.

"See? They hang upside down all day. They even sleep upside down."

"You're upside down," said Stink.

"What do they eat?" asked Dad.

"It says here they eat leaf-cutter ants and fire-bellied toads," Judy read.

"That should be easy," said Stink.

"Tell you what, Judy," said Dad. "Let's take a ride over to the pet store. I'm not saying we'll get a sloth, but it's always fun to look around. Maybe it'll even help me think of a five-letter word for fish that starts with *M* for my crossword puzzle."

"Let's all go," said Mom.

When they arrived at Fur & Fangs, Judy saw snakes and parrots, hermit crabs and guppies. She even saw a five-letter fish word beginning with *M*—a black molly.

"Do you have any two-toed sloths?" she asked the pet store lady.

"Sorry. Fresh out," said the lady.

"How about a newt or a turtle?" asked Dad.

"Did you see the hamsters?" asked Mom.

"Never mind," said Judy. "There's nothing from the rain forest here."

"Maybe they have a stinkbug," Stink said.

"One's enough," said Judy, narrowing her eyes at Stink. They picked out a squeaky mouse toy for Mouse. When they went to pay for it, Judy noticed a green plant with teeth sitting on the counter. "What's that?" she asked the pet store lady.

"A Venus flytrap," the lady said. "It's not an animal, but it doesn't cost much, and it's easy to take care of. See these things that look like mouths with teeth? Each one closes like a trap door. It eats bugs around the house. Like flies and ants, that sort of thing. You can feed it a little raw hamburger too."

"Rare," said Judy Moody.

"Cool," said Stink.

"Good idea," said Mom.

"Sold," said Dad.

Judy set her new pet on her desk, where the angle of sunlight hit it just right. Mouse watched from the bottom bunk, with one eye open.

"I can't wait to take my new pet to school tomorrow for Share and Tell," Judy told Stink. "It's just like a rare plant from the rain forest."

"It is?" Stink asked.

"Sure," said Judy. "Just think. There could be a medicine hiding right here in these funny green teeth. When I'm a doctor, I'm going to study plants like this and discover cures for ucky diseases."

"What are you going to name it?" asked Stink.

"I don't know yet," said Judy.

"You could call it Bughead, since it likes bugs."

"Nah," said Judy.

Judy watered her new pet. She sprinkled Gro-Fast on the soil. When Stink left, she sang songs to it. "I know an old lady who swallowed a fly. . . ." She sang till the old lady swallowed a horse.

She still couldn't think of a good name.
Rumpelstiltskin? Too long. Thing? Maybe.

"Stink!" she called. "Go get me a fly."

"How am I going to catch a fly?" asked Stink.

"One fly. I'll give you a dime." Stink ran down to
the window behind the couch and brought back a fly.

"Gross! That fly is dead."

"It was going to be dead in a minute anyway."

Judy scooped up the dead fly with the tip of her
ruler and dropped it into one of the mouths. In a flash,
the trap closed around the fly. Just like the pet store
lady said.

"Rare!" said Judy.

"Snap! Trap!" Stink said, adding sound effects.

"Go get me an ant. A live one this time."

Here's one...

...a real beauty!

Here anty, anty!

No way!

Snap! Trap!

Urp!

Stink wanted to see the Venus flytrap eat again, so he got his sister an ant. "Snap! Trap!" said Judy and Stink when another trap closed.

"Double rare," Judy said.

"Stink, go catch me a spider or something."

"I'm tired of catching bugs," said Stink.

"Then go ask Mom or Dad if we have any raw hamburger."

Stink frowned.

"Please, pretty please with bubble-gum ice cream on top?" Judy begged. Stink didn't budge. "I'll let you feed it this time."

Stink ran to the kitchen and came back with a hunk of raw hamburger. He plopped a big glob of hamburger into an open trap.

"That's way too much!" Judy yelled, but it was too late. The mouth snap-trapped around it, hamburger oozing out of its teeth. In a blink, the whole arm drooped, collapsing in the dirt.

"You killed it! You're in trouble, Stink. MOM! DAD!" Judy called.

Judy showed her parents what happened. "Stink killed my Venus flytrap!"

"I didn't mean to," said Stink. "The trap closed really fast!"

"It's not dead. It's digesting," said Dad.

"The jaws will probably open by tomorrow morning," said Mom.

"Maybe it's just sleeping or something," said Stink.

"Or something," said Judy.

My Smelly Pet

Tomorrow morning came. The jaws were still closed. Judy tried teasing it with a brand new ant. "Here you go," she said in her best squeaky baby voice. "You like ants, don't you?" The jaws did not open one tiny centimeter. The plant did not move one trigger hair.

Judy gave up. She carefully lodged the plant in the bottom of her backpack. She'd take it to school, stinky, smelly glob of hamburger and all.

On the bus, Judy showed Rocky her new pet. "I couldn't wait to show everybody how it eats. Now it won't even move. And it smells."

"Open Sesame!" said Rocky, trying some magic words. Nothing happened.

"Maybe," said Rocky, "the bus will bounce it open."

"Maybe," said Judy. But even the bouncing of the bus did not make her new pet open up.

"If this thing dies, I'm stuck with Mouse for MY FAVORITE PET," Judy said.

Mr. Todd said first thing, "Okay, class, take out your Me collage folders. I'll pass around old magazines, and you can spend the next half-hour cutting out pictures for your collages. You still have over three weeks, but I'd like to see how everybody's doing."

Her Me collage folder! Judy had been so busy with her new pet, she had forgotten to bring her folder to school.

Judy Moody sneaked a peek at Frank Pearl's folder. He had cut out pictures of macaroni (favorite food?), ants (favorite pet?), and shoes. Shoes? Frank Pearl's best friend was a pair of shoes?

Judy looked down at the open backpack under her desk. The jaws were still closed. Now her whole backpack was smelly. Judy took the straw from her juice box and poked at the Venus flytrap. No luck. It would never open in time for Share and Tell!

"Well?" Frank asked.

"Well, what?"

"Are you going to come?"

"Where?"

"My birthday party. A week from Saturday. All the boys from our class are coming. And Adrian and Sandy from next door."

Judy Moody did not care if the president himself was coming. She sniffed her backpack. It stunk like a skunk!

"What's in your backpack?" Frank asked.

"None of your beeswax," Judy said.

"It smells like dead tuna fish!" Frank Pearl said. Judy hoped her Venus flytrap would come back to life and bite Frank Pearl before he ever had another birthday.

Mr. Todd came over. "Judy, you haven't cut out any pictures. Do you have your folder?"

"I did—I mean—it was—then—well—no," said Judy. "I got a new pet last night."

"Don't tell me," said Mr. Todd. "Your new pet ate your Me collage folder."

"Not exactly. But it did eat one dead fly and one live ant. And then a big glob of . . ."

"Next time try to remember to bring your folder to school, Judy. And please, everyone, keep homework away from animals!"

"My new pet's not an animal, Mr. Todd," Judy said. "And it doesn't eat homework. Just bugs and raw hamburger." She pulled the Venus flytrap from her backpack. Judy could not believe her eyes! Its arm was no longer droopy. The stuck trap was now wide open, and her plant was looking hungry.

"It's MY FAVORITE PET," said Judy. "Meet Jaws!"

Activity Central

Defined Online

In the chapter "My Favorite Pet," Judy asks Stink to get some bugs. At first Stink does not budge. If you don't know the meaning of the word *budge,* you can use an online dictionary to look up the meaning.

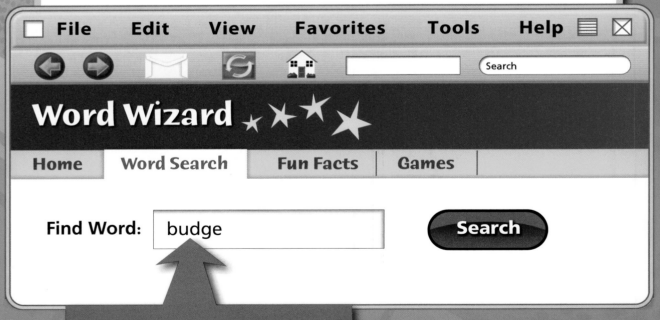

File   Edit   View   Favorites   Tools   Help

Search

Word Wizard ★ ★ ★ ★

Home   Word Search   Fun Facts   Games

Find Word: budge

Search

In the search box, type the word you want to look up. Click on the "Search" button or press the "Enter" key on the keyboard.

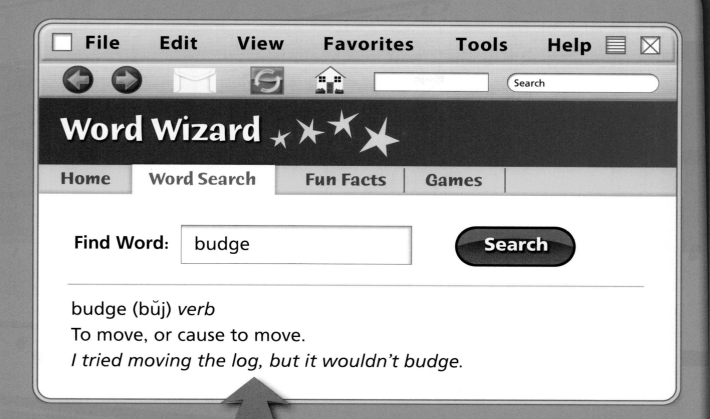

File   Edit   View   Favorites   Tools   Help

Word Wizard ★★★★

Home   **Word Search**   Fun Facts   Games

Find Word: budge   **Search**

budge (bŭj) *verb*
To move, or cause to move.
I tried moving the log, but it wouldn't budge.

Read the entry to find out what the word means. If there is more than one entry for a word, choose the meaning that matches the way the word is used in the selection.

Read the sentences. Use an online dictionary to find the meanings of the underlined words.

1. When they finished their meal at the restaurant, they paid for it at the <u>counter</u>.

2. The old mansion had a <u>trap door</u>.

3. The leaves of the plant were <u>droopy</u>.

4. The <u>trigger</u> hairs on the plant swayed toward the insect.

Let's Make Something Very Clear

Definitions

Good writers add definitions to explain the meaning of words that may not be familiar to their readers.

No Definition	Strong Definition
The Venus flytrap is a carnivorous plant.	The Venus flytrap is a carnivorous plant because it eats meat.

Why is the strong definition better? The word *carnivorous* is explained within the sentence as a word to describe something that eats meat.

Connecting Words

Good writers add connecting words, such as *also*, *another*, *and*, *more*, and *but* to link their ideas and make them clear to their readers.

Weak Link	Strong Link
You can feed a Venus flytrap flies and ants if you want to catch them. You can feed it hamburger.	You can feed a Venus flytrap flies and ants if you want to catch them. You can also feed it hamburger.

Why is the strong link better? It uses the word *also* to show that flies, ants, and hamburger are all foods you can feed a Venus flytrap.

Reflect On Your Writing

Choose a piece of your writing from Unit 4. Look it over. Ask yourself these questions:

▶ Where can I add definitions to explain the meaning of words that may not be familiar to my audience?

▶ Where can I use connecting words such as *and*, *but*, *then*, *also*, *another*, and *more* to link ideas?

Edit your writing to add definitions and connecting words to link ideas.

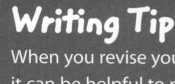

Writing Tip

When you revise your writing, it can be helpful to read your writing out loud. Hearing what you have written can help you notice places for improvement.

Ram's Angry Horns
A Myth from Nigeria

retold by Myka-Lynne Sokoloff
illustrated by Cindy Revell

◆◇◆◇◆◇◆◇◆◇◆◇◆◇◆◇◆◇◆◇◆◇◆

One fine spring day, when the world was new, Ewe gave birth to a lamb. Soon all of the villagers crowded around to admire her new lamb.

"What a handsome thing he is!" said Leopard. Gazelle also looked fondly at the young lamb.

"It's good to have new life in the village," said Elephant.

Hyena joked, "One day soon lamb will be running around the village, butting into everyone's business." The villagers all chuckled at the remark. No one knew how true Hyena's words would turn out to be.

Finally, the villagers left the new mother to rest peacefully with her lamb. "You will be called Ram," Ewe baaed softly. "You are the handsomest baby in all of Africa!"

Indeed, the lamb became more and more
handsome as he grew. In fact, he was so handsome
that he seemed to get his way with everyone, especially
his mother. Ram thought only about himself. He never
stopped to think about others.

In time, the other young animals in the village
became very put out with Ram. They no longer wanted
to play with him. When they saw Ram, the other
animal children ran and hid.

Each day, from morning till night, Ram raced around the village causing trouble. Ram splashed in the water. He sprayed droplets of water on Hyena, who lounged in the sun on the shore. Ram hopped across the river stones. Then he ran boldly up and down Crocodile's back, from the tip of Crocodile's tail to the very end of his nose! He ran through the fields where others had just planted seeds. He rubbed his muddy coat against the clean laundry that hung on the line. He tracked mud through the hut where his mother had just swept the floor.

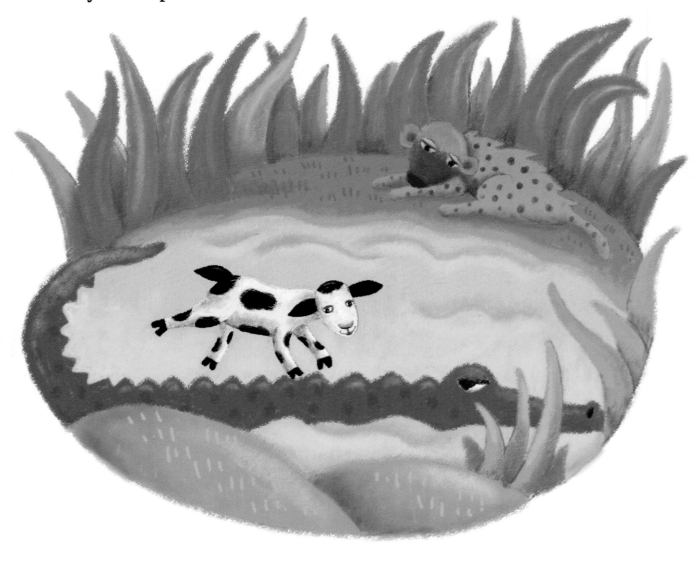

Ewe looked up from her chores and saw all the mischief Ram was making. She baaed gently to make her son stop, but he just pretended not to hear her. Ewe bleated and cried more strongly, until soon she was bellowing deeply and loudly. Ram continued to ignore his mother.

Ram had no friends, and his mother didn't know what to do with her selfish child. She truly wished he would learn some manners, but she had spoiled him beyond repair. Each time Ram misbehaved, the villagers shivered. They waited nervously for Ewe's loud bellows to begin.

Zebra covered her ears. Elephant winced in pain. Crocodile swam away. Flamingo flapped her wings wildly. Hyena would have laughed, but he didn't find Ram's tricks particularly funny.

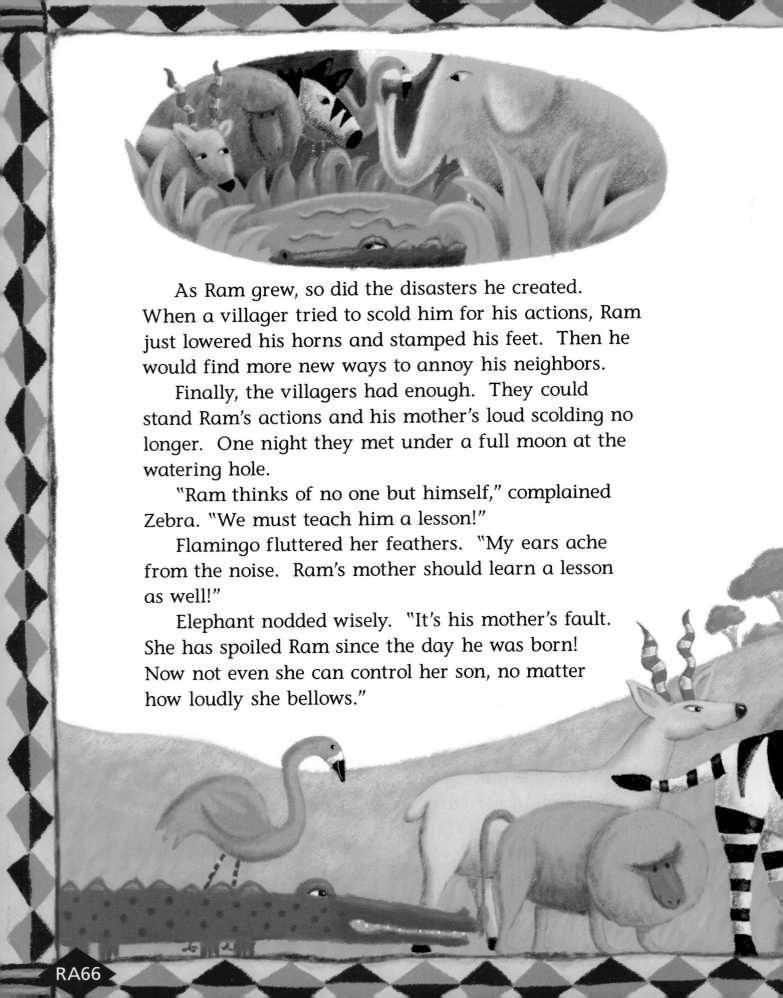

As Ram grew, so did the disasters he created. When a villager tried to scold him for his actions, Ram just lowered his horns and stamped his feet. Then he would find more new ways to annoy his neighbors.

Finally, the villagers had enough. They could stand Ram's actions and his mother's loud scolding no longer. One night they met under a full moon at the watering hole.

"Ram thinks of no one but himself," complained Zebra. "We must teach him a lesson!"

Flamingo fluttered her feathers. "My ears ache from the noise. Ram's mother should learn a lesson as well!"

Elephant nodded wisely. "It's his mother's fault. She has spoiled Ram since the day he was born! Now not even she can control her son, no matter how loudly she bellows."

"We have no choice," Baboon said. "We must send Ram and his mother away from the village. Otherwise, our homes and our children will constantly be in harm's way."

Soon the villagers agreed on a solution. They packed up Ram, his mother, and their belongings. They all formed a parade to escort Ram and Ewe to the edge of town. Ewe and Ram were to speak to no one in the village again.

"Ah, quiet," sighed Leopard as he lay down to doze in the soft, flat grass.

"Now we can get some rest," thought Elephant. It had been so long, she nearly forgot what a nice nap felt like.

"Peace at last," said Crocodile, grinning widely in the river.

The peace did not last long. Although Ram had no friends in the village, now that he was so far from others, he felt lonely. He was bored, too. Even outside of the village, Ewe could control her son no better than she could in the village.

One day Ram pawed at the dirt and kicked the grass. Ram got angrier and angrier as he stood there, feeling sorry for himself.

As Ram stared at the ground, he noticed something shiny. It was a piece of glass. That gave him an idea. He knew how he would get even with the animals in the village!

Ram held the glass so that it caught the sun's rays. It shone brightly on a clump of dried grass. Very quickly, the grass grew warm. Finally, it began to burn. Ram blew on the little flame with all his might.

Next, Ram shook his horned head as fast as he could to make the flames grow higher. He stood back and rubbed his hooves together with glee.

The flames raced toward the village. The fire burned up the grass where Leopard napped in the warm sun. Leopard escaped just in time! The flames licked the leafy trees where Cheetah liked to climb. Fortunately, Cheetah was off doing laundry at the river, so he wasn't hurt. Soon the fire dashed toward the huts that circled the center of the village.

"I smell smoke," Hyena giggled nervously.

Flamingo pointed one wing at the ball of fire that headed straight in their direction.

"Quick, everyone! We must do something!" screamed Baboon.

Elephant trumpeted to call the villagers together. Then she raced to the watering hole and filled her trunk to spray the flames. The other villagers carried baskets and gourds of water to put out the fire. By the time they finished, the watering hole was nearly dry. When night fell, the flames were out, but little remained of the village. Once again, the villagers met under the full moon.

"We put up with Ram's tricks when he was young," Leopard complained. "His mother just got noisier and noisier. We covered our ears to block the sound."

Baboon nodded. "Now Ram has ruined our food and burned our homes."

"We must send Ram and his mother even farther away," Elephant said. The villagers agreed, sadly, for they did not want to harm their neighbors.

The villagers put their heads together and came up with a plan. They used a fallen tree trunk to build a giant seesaw. Ram and Ewe stood on one end. Elephant and Cheetah jumped on the other end. Ram and his mother flew high up into the clouds.

Now you may be wondering what happened to Ram and his mother. If you look and listen carefully next time a thunderstorm comes, you will find the answer in the sky.

Those lightning bolts? That's just Ram tossing balls of fire around the sky with his angry horns. That noise you call thunder? That's his mother, bellowing at her naughty son.

The sky will be their home forever. For that is where they belong, far away from the village, where they would surely make more trouble!

Read It! Record It!

Myths, such as *Ram's Angry Horns,* were first told by parents to their children or by storytellers a very long time ago.

Have you ever listened to a storyteller or to a story read aloud on a CD or podcast? These stories are told or read by someone who has practiced to make the story fun to listen to.

Choose a story or poem to read aloud.

1. Read the story or poem aloud a few times. Try out some different voices to make your characters come alive. Don't read too fast or too slowly.

2. Once you have practiced reading the story or poem, make a recording.

3. Listen to the recording, and make sure you like the way it sounds. If it's not as good as you would like, record it again.

4. Draw some pictures to make the details of the story or poem clearer to your listeners.

Be sure you
- Speak clearly.
- Vary your speed.
- Use lots of expression.

Then play your recording for your class and display your pictures. If your teacher has a class website, you may be able to post your recording and pictures for your friends and family to enjoy. Get ready to take a bow!

What Happens in the End?

A good story makes it easy for the reader to get to know the characters and what happens to them. A good story has a problem and gets the reader interested in how the characters solve the problem. Good writers make sure to tell how the problem is solved.

Ram's Angry Horns is fun to read because it has interesting characters that have to solve a problem. What is the problem? What happens at the end of *Ram's Angry Horns*? Does the ending tell how the problem is solved?

Reflect On Your Writing

Choose a story you wrote in Unit 5. As you read over your story, ask yourself these questions:

- What problem do the characters have?

- Did I organize the events in an order that makes sense?

- Is the problem solved in the end?

If you answer *No* to any of the questions, edit your story.

Make Your Mark

In the next section of this magazine you will discover a world of achievers. You'll read about a runner who crosses America in a 1928 foot race and a mountain climber who relies on his sense of touch. A neighborhood that comes together to save a dog may inspire you.

You'll read poems and articles about sports, spellers, and inventions, and you'll do lots of fun activities.

So, on your mark…get set…turn the page!

Jesse Owens, Six World Records
32 USA

Make Your Mark

Paca and the Beetle

A Folktale from Brazil

A beautiful red, blue, gold, and green macaw watched a brown beetle as it crawled across the jungle floor.

"Where are you going, my friend?" Macaw called out.

"I am going to the sea."

Just then, a paca skittered by. "You?" Paca laughed. "You're so slow it will take you a hundred years!" Macaw looked down. "You shouldn't brag, Paca. Why don't you race him? I'll give a new coat to whoever first reaches the big tree beside the river."

Paca laughed harder. "This is no race!" he giggled. "You may as well give me the yellow coat and black spots of a jaguar right now!"

"I will race," Beetle said. "If I win, I would like a coat like yours, Macaw."

Paca dashed away. Then he thought, "Why should I hurry? I am so much faster than slow Beetle. I can take my time." He smiled, thinking of the fine new coat he would soon wear.

When Paca neared the tree, however, he was amazed to see Beetle on a branch waiting for him.

Scarlet macaws are found throughout South America. These spectacular birds are about three feet long from head to tail.

4

The Ceiba borer, or "living jewel," of Brazil is one of the world's most beautiful insects. People use the wing covers of its shell in jewelry.

Paca gasped. "How did *you* get here?" he demanded.

"I flew," Beetle answered with a smile.

"You have wings?" Paca asked.

Macaw answered. "Beetle doesn't brag about his wings, but he can use them when he needs to. Beetle is the winner."

Paca hung his head and slunk away, still wearing the brown coat with white spots he had always had. Then Macaw smiled at Beetle, and Beetle's hard back began to shine with the colors of Macaw's feathers. The beetle's shell has gleamed with a rainbow of colors ever since.

The spotted paca lives in the jungles of Brazil. It weighs between twelve and twenty-five pounds and is the world's second-largest rodent.

Discuss the Selection

- What is the moral, or lesson, in this story? Which story details explain this lesson?
- Compare and contrast "Paca and the Beetle" and *The Raven, An Inuit Myth*, in Unit 5. How are the characters, settings, and plots alike and different?

5

The Foot Race Across America

Back in 1926, in the hills around Foyil, Oklahoma, the jackrabbits must have gotten used to the sound of Andy Payne running by. The Cherokee teenager was almost as fast as they were.

Andy loved to run. After he finished the morning chores on his family's farm, he ran five miles to school. He often got there before his brothers and sisters, who arrived on horseback. "I just . . . had a knack for being able to cover the ground on foot," he later explained. In those days, Andy won prizes in many track tournaments, especially long-distance events like the mile. His biggest race would be much longer than that, though.

"Runners Wanted"

After he graduated from high school in 1927, Andy, now age twenty, went to Los Angeles, California, to look for a job. Work turned out to be hard to find. One day he read an ad in a newspaper that would change his life. "Runners wanted," the ad said. An International Trans-Continental Foot Race was going to take place in March. The race would start in Los Angeles and end across the country in New York City. That was a distance of over 3,400 miles. The winner would receive twenty-five thousand dollars!

The 1920s were already known for crazy contests. There were dance marathons, six-day bicycle races, even people setting records for sitting on flagpoles. A man named C. C. Pyle planned the foot race to follow the recently built Route 66, a road that stretched from Los Angeles to Chicago.

Andy Payne was excited. He felt he had as good a chance to win as anyone. The prize money would help his parents pay for their farm. It might also help persuade his girlfriend, Vivian Shaddox, to marry him.

The Starting Line

Andy hurried back to Oklahoma. He talked his father and local officials into lending him the $125 he needed to enter the race. Then he returned to California to train. After three weeks of running and getting into shape there, he felt ready.

On the morning of March 4, 1928, Andy lined up with nearly two hundred other runners at the starting line. They came from across the United States as well as from other countries, including Finland, Switzerland, Canada, and Italy. They were as young as sixteen and as old as sixty-three. A few were already famous for competing in marathons and other long-distance races. One was the son of a millionaire. Most, however, were poor. In 1928, an average factory worker earned $1,200 a year. Winning the prize money would be like receiving twenty years' salary.

Finally, the great football player "Red" Grange gave the signal. Boom! All 199 men sprang forward, each one dreaming of victory in New York City.

Map labels: NY, New York, FINISH, PA, OH, IN, Chicago, IL, MO, Oklahoma City, OK, CA, Los Angeles, START, AZ, NM, TX

Legend: — Foot race route

Over Mountains and Deserts

The first day of the race was the easiest. All the runners made it to the town of Puente, California, seventeen miles away. But it would soon get harder. The runners had to climb steep Cajon (kuh HOHN) Pass, and then deal with the intense heat of the Mojave (moh HAH vay) Desert. By the 12th of March—one week into the race—more than fifty runners had dropped out, tired by the steep climbs and blistered by the desert sun.

A record was kept of the runners' time for each day. Surprising many of the more famous runners was number forty-three, Andy Payne. Andy was running in third place.

As the runners left behind California for Arizona, they faced even tougher climbs. By March 21st, more than half of the original 199 had dropped out, including the man who had been in first place, the South African long-distance champion, Arthur Newton.

The runners had also discovered that C. C. Pyle, the race organizer, was not a man of his word. Instead of the big meals they enjoyed at the start of the race, they were now served poor stews. Often, Pyle's big caravan, nicknamed "America," was late with the tents, cots, and blankets—which were never washed. Then the runners were forced to sleep in barns or stables.

Andy Payne was having his own troubles. He had tonsillitis and a fever. But he kept up the pace. After the runners had made their way through the snow and mud of northern Texas, Andy entered his home state of Oklahoma in the lead.

The Bunion Derby

By now the foot race was attracting lots of attention. The newspapers had begun to call it "The Bunion Derby." But Andy was lucky—he didn't have bunions, swelling of the big toes. In Oklahoma City, Andy told a cheering crowd and the governor of the state, "Hope to see you in New York." When he ran through his hometown of Foyil, he took a few minutes to visit his girlfriend, Vivian, and his family. And he bought a new pair of running shoes.

Andy was becoming friendly with some of the other runners. One, John Salo, had adopted a dog in Arizona named Blisters, and ran with Blisters all the way to Missouri. Phillip Granville, a Canadian, believed he could win the race by walking, then changed his mind and began to run. Andy's closest friend was also his closest rival, an Englishman named Peter Gavuzzi. They traded the lead from Oklahoma to Ohio. That was where Peter, more than six hours ahead of Andy, had to drop out because of a toothache.

With a thousand miles left to go, Andy Payne took over first place for good.

The Finish Line

By the third week of May, the runners were closing in on New York City. The daily distances were getting longer. One day, the men ran nearly seventy-five miles. C. C. Pyle, the race organizer, was broke. It wasn't certain that he would be able to pay the winners the prize money. But on May 26, 1928, the Bunioneers, as the fifty-five remaining runners were now called, came plodding in to New York's Madison Square Garden. Even though they had been running for eighty-four days, they had to keep running, circling the arena for another twenty miles before the race was over.

In the end, C. C. Pyle did come up with the money. It took 573 hours, 4 minutes, and 34 seconds, but Andy Payne achieved his dream. He won the $25,000 first prize. John Salo (and Blisters) won the $10,000 second prize. Phillip Granville, the Canadian walker, won the third prize of $5,000.

Andy took the train back to Oklahoma. True to his word, he paid what his family owed on their farm. In 1929, he married Vivian Shaddox. That year there was a second Trans-Continental foot race, this one going in the opposite direction, from New York City to Los Angeles. Andy did not take part. The winner was Peter Gavuzzi, his sore tooth all healed.

Today, people still remember Andy Payne for his remarkable achievement. Every May an "Andy Payne Bunion Run" marathon takes place in Oklahoma City. And if you happen to be traveling on Route 66 by Andy's hometown of Foyil, you'll see a life-size statue of Andy, doing what he loved to do. Running.

Madison Square Garden occupied this building from 1925 to 1968.

Fast Track

by Nikki Grimes

When the whistle blows
I am ready and set
and no one can tell me
I am too anything
or less than enough.
I am a tornado of legs and feet
and warm wind whipping past
everyone else on the track
and all that's on my mind
is scissoring through
the finish line.

Ode to My Shoes

by Francisco X. Alarcón

my shoes
rest
all night
under my bed

tired
they stretch
and loosen
their laces

wide open
they fall asleep
and dream
of walking

they revisit
the places
they went to
during the day

and wake up
cheerful
relaxed
so soft

Discuss Poetry
- The first poet uses a **metaphor.** What does she say a runner *is*? How does this help you imagine what it's like to be the runner?
- The second poet uses **personification**. Which human traits does he give to a pair of shoes? How do they look, act, and feel?

Design a Stamp

USA 37
CESAR E. CHAVEZ

You need a stamp to send a letter. But stamps have another purpose. They are often used to honor people's achievements.

Design a stamp to honor Andy Payne and his race across the United States, or choose another person whose achievement you would like to honor.

Make sure you include the following features in your stamp design:

1. The **country:** All United States stamps have the letters *USA*.

2. The **value:** Include a number that shows how much the stamp costs.

3. A **picture:** Show a picture of the person you are honoring, or show a place or object connected with the achievement.

4. A **name or description:** Include the person's name or a brief description of the achievement. For example, you might use the words *World's fastest runner* for an athlete who set a record.

32 USA
Jesse Owens, Six World Records

American holly 32 USA

33 USA
The "Shot Heard 'Round the World"

USA 15c
HELEN KELLER
ANNE SULLIVAN

Sojourner Truth
22
Black Heritage USA

Add -ion

When the suffix *-ion* is added to a verb, the new word
is a noun. It names the action that the verb shows.

Example: Paca didn't **act** kindly toward Beetle.
His **action** made him look foolish in the end!

Go on an *-ion* hunt. Read each pair of sentences.
Find a word in the first sentence that you can add *-ion* to. Use the
noun you form to complete the second sentence on a separate
piece of paper.

1. Do you suggest that we run across the United
   States? What a silly _____
   that is!

2. The runners had nothing to protect them
   as they ran through the desert. People need ___
   from the desert sun.

3. Signs were used to direct the runners. They ran
   in an east-west _____ across the country.

4. Inspect the map on page 9 to see the race route. During your
   _____ , count how many states Andy Payne ran through.

5. I predict that you will win a race one day.
   If my _____ comes true, I'll congratulate you!

17

And the

In "Paca and the Beetle," you read about a race between two very different creatures. Write your own story about a contest between two animals that are opposites. For example, the contest might be between the tallest animal and the shortest animal in a jungle. Or the contest might be between the strongest animal and the weakest animal on a farm. Remember, the winner of the contest doesn't have to be the one you'd expect to win.

Winner Is...

Story Tips

- Introduce the characters and the setting, or where and when the story takes place.
- Tell about the contest. What is it supposed to prove?
- Describe what happens during the contest.
- Show who wins the contest, and tell why.

The POWER of Magnets

Chances are there's a magnet on your refrigerator. It's probably holding up a photo, a drawing, or some other piece of paper. Have you noticed that the magnet sticks to the refrigerator but not to the paper? Do you know why?

This refrigerator magnet is actually pulling on the refrigerator.

A magnet attracts objects with iron in them. The refrigerator door is probably made of steel, which is made from iron. Paper has no iron in it. That's why the magnet doesn't stick to it.

If you ever spill a box of pins, a good way to pick them up is with a magnet. The magnet will pull the pins toward it. Most of the pins will stick to the ends, or poles, of the magnet. That's because the poles are the most powerful part of a magnet.

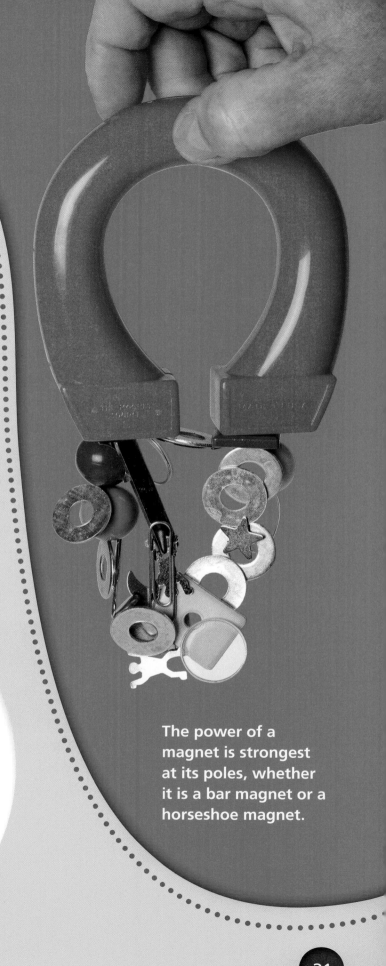

The power of a magnet is strongest at its poles, whether it is a bar magnet or a horseshoe magnet.

Some magnets are bars. Other magnets are shaped like horseshoes.

Poles and Fields

A magnet has a north pole and a south pole. What happens if you try to touch the north pole of one magnet to the south pole of another magnet? They'll stick together. Opposite poles attract each other.

Will two north poles or two south poles stick together? No, they won't. In fact, they will repel, or push each other away. Like poles repel each other.

This special force that attracts or repels is called magnetic force. A magnet's force is not felt just at its poles. A magnet creates a whole area, or field, of force around it.

Do you want to see a magnetic field? Sprinkle iron filings around a magnet. The iron filings will form a pattern of lines. They show the magnetic field, where the magnet's force works. The lines are closest together at the poles, where the force is strongest.

A magnetic field is invisible, but these iron pieces show where it is.

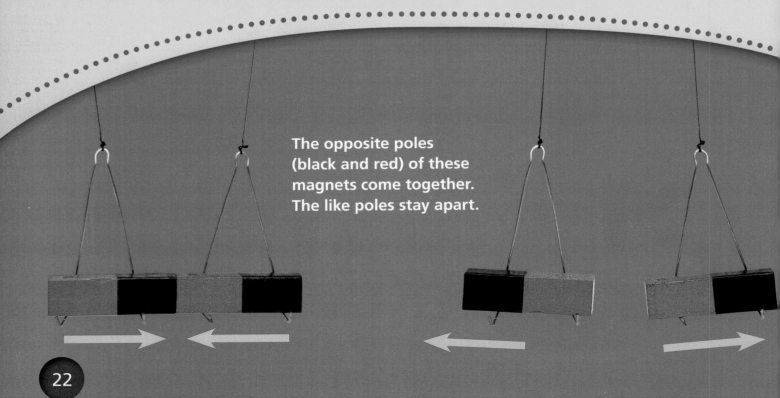

The opposite poles (black and red) of these magnets come together. The like poles stay apart.

Electromagnets: Turn Them On, Turn Them Off

Some magnets can be turned on and off. If you need a magnet whose force you can control like this, you want an electromagnet. In an electromagnet, wire is wrapped around metal. Electricity can flow through the wire. When you turn the electricity on, the metal becomes a magnet! It is an electromagnet. When you turn the electricity off, the metal stops being a magnet.

Junkyards use huge electromagnets to move old cars. A special crane turns electricity on. That turns a core of metal into a magnet. The car sticks to the magnet, and the crane moves the car with ease. Then the electricity is turned off, and the magnet turns back into plain metal. The car drops into place.

Electromagnets are useful for two reasons: They can be powerful enough to move a car, and they can be turned on and off.

Michael Faraday's Electric Idea

In 1820 people first learned about electromagnets. That year one scientist saw a magnetic field produced when electricity ran through a metal wire. His observation made another scientist, Michael Faraday, curious. Faraday asked himself: If electricity can produce a magnetic field, can a magnetic field produce electricity?

Faraday tested his idea. In one experiment, he moved a magnet through a coil of wires. Electricity was produced! In another, he moved the coil of wires around a magnet. Again, electricity was produced.

Faraday's work led to two important inventions: the electric generator and the electric motor. The electric generator produces electricity with a magnetic field. The electric motor uses electricity to run things. Now people could use magnets to make electricity to do their work for them!

Electric Generators

Generate means "produce or make." An electric generator uses a magnetic field and moving wire coils to produce electricity, just as Michael Faraday discovered.

A power company near your home builds generators. Electricity from these generators comes through power lines into your home. It lets you turn on lights, watch TV, and listen to music. Think of all the times you use electricity. You are using electricity produced in a magnetic field.

Every time you turn on a light switch, electricity comes through a wire. Every time you plug in a cord, electricity comes through the wire. Remember, too, that electricity creates a magnetic field. So every time electricity comes through a wire in your home, it produces a magnetic field. How many magnetic fields do you think are in your home?

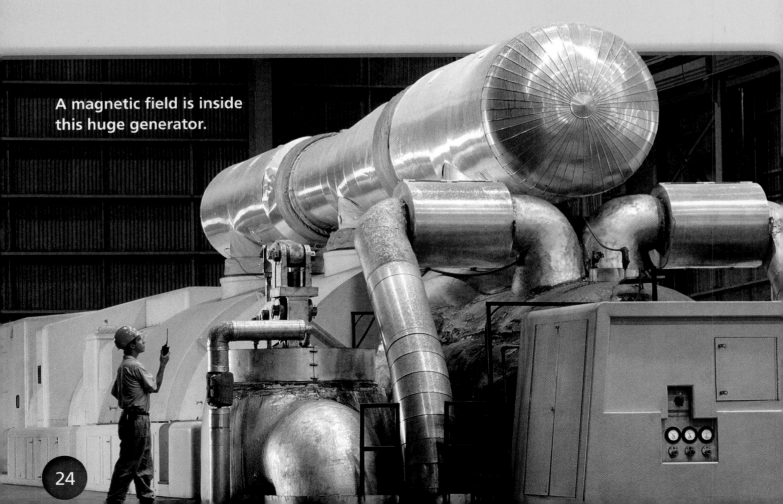

A magnetic field is inside this huge generator.

Electric Motors

Some electricity that comes into your home is used to power electric motors. An electric motor uses electricity to run things. When you plug in and turn on a hair dryer or a fan, an electric motor makes it work.

Some electric motors get their power from batteries. When you put a battery in a watch or a CD player, an electric motor makes it work.

Think about all the toys and tools in your home that have electric motors. Inside each electric motor is a magnet and its magnetic field. How many magnetic fields in electric motors do you think are in your home?

Batteries like these give power to electric motors.

Remember that magnets are not just on your refrigerator door. Magnets help provide the power you use every day.

ELECTRO

You may not know it, but you live with electromagnets all around you. Here are just a few examples.

Ding-dong! Pressing a doorbell turns an electromagnet on. The magnet makes a striker or arm move. It hits a bell, and the doorbell rings.

Did you know that electromagnets help you dry your hair? Any machine with an electric motor uses an electromagnet to turn working parts on and off. So a blow dryer, vacuum cleaner, refrigerator, washing machine, and radio all have electromagnets.

MAGNETS
AND YOU

Electromagnets even help you have fun!

A computer uses electromagnets too. They help store information on the computer's hard drive so you can find it later.

Music pumps out of a stereo's speakers because of electromagnets. Inside, the cone has a coil attached to it. Around that is a magnet. Electricity creates a magnetic field. This vibrates, or shakes, the coil. The cone moves, too. That's what makes the sounds you hear.

Science Fair Project

by Carol Diggory Shields

PURPOSE:

The purpose of my project this year
Is to make my brother disappear.

HYPOTHESIS:

The world would be a better place
If my brother vanished without
a trace.

MATERIALS:

3 erasers
White-out
Disappearing ink
1 younger brother
1 kitchen sink

PROCEDURE:

Chop up the erasers.
Add the white-out and the ink.
Rub it on the brother.
While he's standing in the sink.

RESULTS:

The kid was disappearing!
I had almost proved my theorem!
When all at once my mom
came home
And made me re-appear him.

CONCLUSION:

Experiment a failure.
My brother is still here.
But I'm already planning
For the science fair *next* year.

28

magnet

by Valerie Worth

This small
Flat horseshoe
Is sold for
A toy: we are
Told that it
Will pick up pins
And it does, time
After time; later
It lies about,
Getting its red
Paint chipped, being

Offered pins less
Often, until at
Last we leave it
Alone: then
It leads its own
Life, trading
Secrets with
The North Pole,
Reading
Invisible messages
From the sun.

Discuss Poetry

Compare and contrast form in these two poems. How does each poet arrange her words? Notice capitalization, punctuation, rhyme, and line breaks.

Make a Magnet

Amaze your friends! Tell them you can pick up one paper clip with another without clipping them together. It's not magic. It's magnetism!

> ### Materials
> 1 magnet
> 1 large paper clip
> 1 small paper clip

1. Straighten out the large paper clip. Set it on a table so it's flat.

2. Hold one end of the paper clip down with a fingertip.

3. Hold the magnet in your other hand. Gently, but firmly, slide the magnet along the paper clip from one end to the other. Then lift the magnet up and away from the paper clip.

4. Repeat Step 3 about ten times. Always stroke the magnet in the same direction.

5. Carefully pick up the magnetized paper clip. Use its tip to pick up the small paper clip.

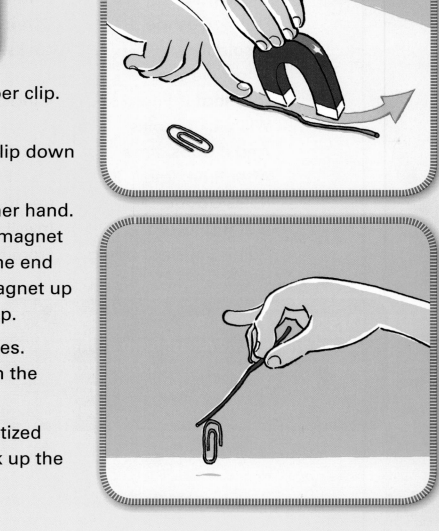

Do the Magnet Jump

Did you know you can make metal objects "jump"?

1. Tape a ruler onto a table so it won't move.

2. Tape the magnet so one end is facing the beginning of the ruler.

3. Place the pin along the ruler an inch or two away from the magnet. Gently nudge the object toward the magnet until it "jumps" toward the magnet.

4. Record the mark where the object was right before its jump.

5. Repeat Steps 3 and 4 with the other objects. Record the distance each one jumps.

After you do the activity, explain the directions to a classmate.

Materials
1 centimeter ruler
1 magnet
tape
a straight pin
a small and a
large paper clip
a nail

Object	Distance "Jumped"
straight pin	
small paper clip	
large paper clip	
nail	

Wow!

What an Invention!

You've been reading about useful inventions—the magnet, the electromagnet, the electric motor, and others. Think about something *you'd* like to invent. What would it do?

Your invention can be simple or complicated. It can be useful or silly. It can even be something that already exists but that you wish you had invented.

Write a description of your invention and what it does. Then draw a picture of it.

Invention Tips

- State your invention's name.
- Make a drawing of your invention and label its parts.
- Write a description of what your invention does and how it works.

Becoming ANYTHING He Wants to Be

*I*magine cold *so* cold that bare skin freezes almost instantly. Imagine wind so strong that it could blow you over and deep icy cracks you might fall into at any moment. Now picture a group of mountain climbers making their way through this environment to the highest spot in the world. One of the climbers is Erik Weihenmayer.

On May 25, 2001, Erik did make it to the top of Mount Everest, the tallest mountain on earth. But Erik could not see the view from the top. He could not even see the snow and ice all around him. He could only feel them because he is blind. Erik is the only blind person ever to reach the top of the world.

On May 25, 2001, Erik became the first blind person to climb to the top of Mount Everest.

A Hard Beginning

Erik was born with a rare eye disease. He could never see very well. By the time he was 13, the disease had made him blind.

People often think of all the things a blind person can't do because he or she can't see. Erik's father encouraged Erik to think about the things he *could* do. Erik learned that lesson well.

It wasn't always easy. At first, Erik was angry when he lost his sight. He refused to learn Braille, a writing and reading system for blind people. He failed math his first year in high school because he could not read the Braille textbook.

Then Erik started wrestling. It was a sport where his blindness did not slow him. He learned Braille, and his grades improved. He became the captain of the wrestling team. One year he won second place in the state wrestling championship.

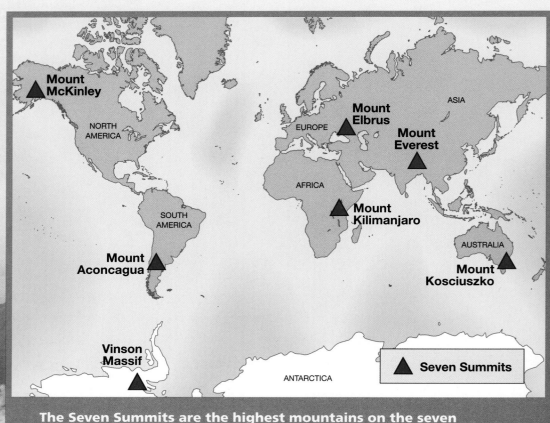

The Seven Summits are the highest mountains on the seven continents. Every mountain climber dreams of climbing them all. Very few achieve this dream.

The Thrill of the Climb

When he was sixteen, Erik went rock climbing for the first time. The experience changed his life. He loved the feel of the wind and the rock under his hands. Different rocks had different textures. This thrilled him and made him want to climb more and more.

Yet Erik did not want only to follow other climbers. Blind people had climbed that way for a long time. Erik wanted to lead. He wanted to find the toeholds and places for his hands by touch. One night, he proved he *could* lead.

He was climbing with a partner, and they finished after dark. The partner had forgotten his helmet light. He could not see to climb down. But Erik could "see" with his hands. He led the climb back down to safety.

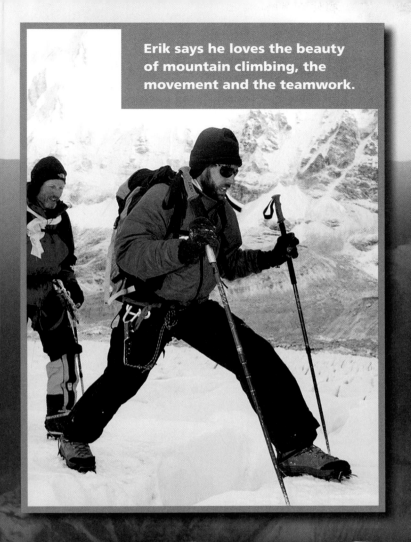

Erik says he loves the beauty of mountain climbing, the movement and the teamwork.

Climbing the Seven Summits

Soon Erik began climbing mountains! He discovered he could use long poles to lean on and help him feel the ground. He could also use his hearing to sense when a cliff was in front of him, or when the ground dropped off. Sometimes climbers in front of him wore bells or tapped their ice axes against rocks to help direct him.

In 1995, Erik climbed to the top of Denali Peak (Mount McKinley) in Alaska. The TV news reported it: a blind man had climbed the tallest mountain in North America! It was the first of the "Seven Summits" that Erik went on to climb. These mountains are the highest on each of the seven continents. Over the next seven years, Erik climbed them all.

Erik wants other people to think about what they can do and not what they cannot do, just as he has done.

A great athlete, Erik competes in tandem bicycle races. Tandem bikes are for two riders.

Not Just a World-Class Climber

Erik didn't stop at mountain climbing. At one time he was a teacher and a wrestling coach. He is also a sky diver. He runs marathon races. He skis. He scuba dives. He does long-distance bike rides. You could never tell Erik that blindness is a handicap.

Now Erik speaks and teaches all around the world. He has written two books. The message in each is that hardships can make us stronger and better people. One of his books is called *Touch the Top of the World*. The story was made into a movie.

Erik also made a movie called *Farther Than the Eye Can See*. It is an adventure film about climbing Mount Everest. Erik used the movie to raise more than half a million dollars for charity. He used his success to help form a group called No Barriers. The group finds ways to help people with disabilities overcome the barriers in their lives.

Today, Erik is trying to help blind people learn to read and write. He wants everyone who cannot see to learn Braille. He speaks all over the world to help make this happen.

Erik was once asked if he believes everything is possible. He answered that there are limits. For example, he cannot drive a car. But, he added, "There are good questions and bad questions in life. The bad questions are what-if questions. 'What if I were smarter, or stronger? What if I could see?' Those are dead-end questions. A good question is, 'How do I do as much as I can with what I have'?"

My Blue Belt Day!

A karate student shows a roundhouse kick.

Just What Is Karate?

Karate is an ancient Asian form of self-defense. It uses no weapons. In fact, *karate* in Japanese means "empty hand." In karate, a person uses kicks, punches, blocks, and hand chops to stop an attacker.

Belt colors show how much karate students have learned. Beginners wear white belts. A student must pass a test to achieve each next belt. The kicks and other moves get harder and more complicated with each level of belt. The highest level is the black belt, the sign of the master.

May 3

Why was I so scared this morning? My stomach was doing flips. You'd think I was facing a cougar instead of a karate test!

I didn't feel scared six months ago. That's when I took my test to earn my green belt. I knew the green belt forms and performed all the kicks and blocks and punches just right.

This morning, though, I didn't feel ready for the blue-belt test. I guess I was unsure about my roundhouse kick. The front kick, side kick, and roundhouse kick all need to be perfect to earn the blue belt.

Just before my test, though, my instructor helped me. *Sensei* Scott said I just needed to focus. He said, "Don't think about earning your blue belt. Just think about each move as you do it."

It worked. I snapped my leg into a front kick. I whipped it out into a side kick. Then I shouted "*Yiah!*" and swung my right leg around for a perfect roundhouse kick.

Now I think that in six months I will be trading my blue belt for purple!

There are different schools of karate.
Most follow this order of belts.

I chop chop chop

by Jack Prelutsky

I chop chop chop without a stop,
I move with great agility.
I break a brick with one quick kick—
Karate… that's the sport for me!

Long Jump

by Kristine O'Connell George

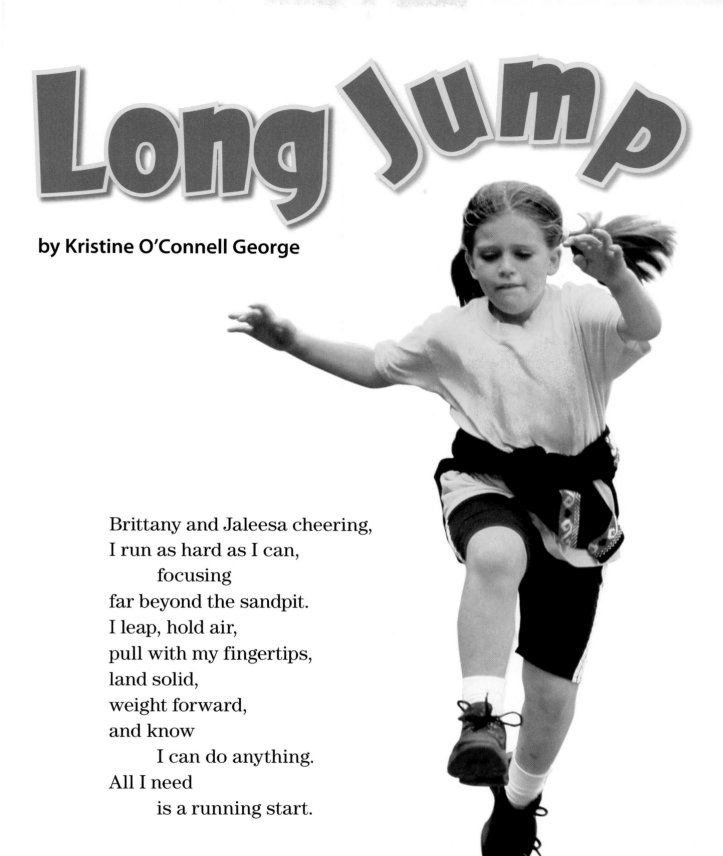

Brittany and Jaleesa cheering,
I run as hard as I can,
        focusing
far beyond the sandpit.
I leap, hold air,
pull with my fingertips,
land solid,
weight forward,
and know
        I can do anything.
All I need
        is a running start.

Interview an ACHIEVER!

Everyone has done something to be proud of. Maybe it was scoring a winning goal in a game. Maybe it was overcoming a fear. Maybe it was helping someone, or it was learning something new. Whatever it was, it's time to share it.

Interview a classmate about an achievement he or she is proud of. Use the list below to guide your interview. Jot your partner's answers down on a sheet of paper. Using your notes, share your partner's achievement with the rest of your class or group. Be sure to speak clearly and to use correct grammar.

1 Achiever's name
2 What achievement makes you the most proud?
3 When did it happen?
4 Where did it happen?
5 How do you feel about what you did?

Build a Word

Many English words have word parts called roots from other languages. If you know the meaning of the root, it will help you understand the meaning of the whole word. Here are the meanings of four roots.

auto = self   graph = write   phon = sound   tele = distance

Example: A **phonograph** is an early record player. It plays **sound** that was **written** down, or recorded, on a disc.

Combine the roots above to make words that answer the riddles below.

1. I'm your name that you **write** your**self**. What am I?

2. I help you hear **sound** from a **distance**. What am I?

3. You use me to **write** a message and send it a **distance**. What am I?

Now make up two words of your own. Use the roots above. Combine them with other words. Your new words do not have to be real. Write a sentence that defines each new word you made.

Example: A **telebird** is a bird that flies a long distance.

Answer Key: 1. autograph; 2. telephone; 3. telegraph

You read about a man who climbed the highest mountain in the world and a girl who earned her blue belt in karate. You may also have a friend, relative, or classmate who accomplished something great. Or maybe you read a story about a character who does something wonderful.

Choose a real person or a story character who achieved a goal. Write a card, congratulating that person on the achievement.

- Decorate the front of the card.
- Inside, write a message. Tell what you think about the person's achievement, as Carrie has done here. Which sentence tells you her purpose for writing this card?
- Include the date on which you are writing.

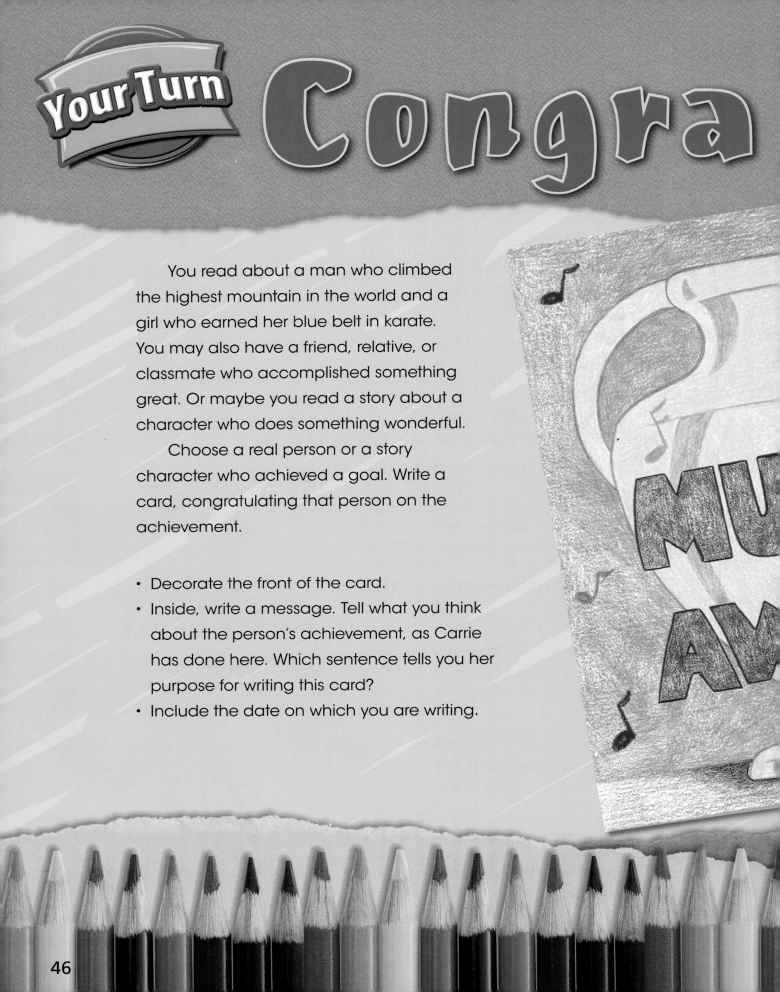

Dear Ava,

May 1

    I am writing this card to congratulate you on winning the school music award. I know you practiced piano every day, and it showed! Your concert was great. You deserve your award.

Your friend,
Carrie

A New TEAM of HEROES

Cast of Characters

Narrator
Lauren
Carla
Hiro
Manny
Gayle

Narrator: Lauren, Carla, Hiro, and Gayle are close friends and members of their third-grade soccer team, the Hawks. Of course, as with any team, some players are better than others.

Lauren: Look at Carla fly down the field! *She's* the reason we win so many games.

Hiro: I wish I could play like her.

Gayle: Me too. But it takes *all* of us to win games, not one player.

Narrator: Late in the fall, just before a big game, a new player joins the Hawks. The coach introduces Manny to everyone. The four friends hope he knows the game.

Gayle: I wonder what kind of player he is.

Carla: Do you think he's good?

Hiro: Why don't you go ask him?

Carla: No, *you* ask!

Lauren: It doesn't matter, since we've got Carla on the field! No one can stop you, Carla.

Carla: Well, I hope he can play.

Gayle: Come on. Let's go practice!

Narrator: A few days later is the big game. Before the start, Manny sits on one end of the bench tying his shoes. The group of friends sit at the other end.

Hiro: This game will be tough.

Gayle: Coach says we can win if we all play hard.

Lauren: That new boy is just sitting by himself.

Carla: Maybe we should talk to him.

Gayle: Let's not worry about it now. It's time for the game to begin.

Narrator: As always, Carla runs onto the field, leading her other teammates.

Hiro, Gayle, and **Lauren** (together): Go, Carla!

Narrator: The game is close. Carla scores two goals, but the other team scores two as well. Every player on the Hawks' bench has had a turn except Manny. When Gayle comes off the field, she decides to sit next to him.

Gayle: Your name is Manny, right? I'm Gayle.

Manny: Hi. You're not a bad soccer player, Gayle.

Gayle: Well, I'm not as good as Carla.

Manny: Yes, she's great!

Narrator: Hiro and Lauren move down the bench.

Hiro: She sure is!

Narrator: Just then, the opposing team scores. Everyone on the bench groans.

Lauren: How could that happen?

Hiro: Now we're losing!

Manny: I've noticed something. Their goalie always moves to her left when we're ready to take a shot. I think I could score on her.

Hiro: Only Carla can beat their goalie.

Gayle: Manny, do you really think you can score on her?

Narrator: Manny nods. Gayle leaps up to talk with the coach.

Lauren: What makes you so sure you can score, Manny?

Manny: I played a lot of soccer at home in Guatemala. I faced goalies like her, and I'm sure I can get past her.

Narrator: Just then, Carla comes to the sideline. Her uniform is stained with grass and dirt. She is gasping for breath.

Carla: I can hardly run any more. And now we're losing by a goal!

Gayle: You'll have some help soon. The coach is going to put Manny in.

Carla: I hope you can play well, Manny.

Manny: I think I can, and I have an idea. When we attack, drive to the goalie's left, and then pass back across to me. I think the net will be open.

Carla: I'll give it a try.

Lauren: Well, Coach says I'm going in the game too. Let's do it!

Narrator: Manny, Carla, and Lauren race onto the field while the others watch.

Hiro: This is amazing! Manny is as good as Carla.

Gayle: He might even be better.

Hiro: Look at them go!

Narrator: On the field, Lauren passes to Carla. Carla races to the goal. The other team's goalie shifts left, just as Manny predicted. Carla passes the ball over to Manny.

Hiro and Gayle (together): Goal! Manny scores!

Narrator: Manny, Carla, and Lauren run to the sideline during the time out. The grinning players are sweaty and breathing hard.

Manny: This time, let's do the same play, but keep running toward the goal, Carla. When they turn to stop me, I'll kick a pass over them back to you.

Carla: We'll need to time our passes perfectly.

Manny: I can do it. Can you?

Carla: I'll try.

Narrator: This time, the coach sends Manny, Carla, and Hiro on the field. With just seconds left in the game, Hiro passes the ball to Manny. Their teammates watch as Manny and Carla dash past the bench toward the goal.

Lauren: Did you see that pass? Carla is a great player!

Gayle: Go, Manny!

Lauren: He kicked it across! Get it, Carla!

Gayle: She has it! She scores! Goal!

Lauren and **Gayle** (together): We win!

Narrator: The players start to run off the field. The players on the bench run to meet them.

Manny: Great shot, Carla!

Carla: Great pass, Manny!

Hiro: Three cheers for Carla!

Lauren: Three cheers for Manny!

All: Three cheers for the HAWKS!

Imagine you are standing on a stage. Hundreds of people in the room are watching you. Millions are seeing you on TV. A man says, "The word is *champion*." It is up to *you* to spell it.

That's how kids in the national spelling bee feel.

Each year, more than 250 kids in elementary and middle school make it to the final bee. They come from all over the United States. A few even come from Canada, the Bahamas, and other countries.

Television helped make spelling bees popular. In 1994 the TV sports station ESPN started showing the national final bee. After that, spelling bees grew fast, and the bees got harder!

To get to the national bee, each speller works up through many smaller bees. A classroom bee might be the first one. The winner then

P·I·O·N

competes against students from other classrooms in the school. One student will win. That winner will spell against students from other local schools. Finally, the Scripps National Spelling Bee is held in Washington, D.C., and shown on TV.

Getting to the finals is hard work. The ones who make it study and practice day after day. They learn base words and roots. That helps them correctly spell words that they have never even heard before.

The spellers face a lot of pressure. To win, they have to spell harder and harder words. One year, a speller fainted at the microphone. Before anyone could help him, he jumped up and correctly spelled his word!

Another year, Katharine Close won by correctly spelling *ursprache*. Most adults don't even know what that word means. (It means "an early language.") Katharine seemed very cool on TV. She just stood with her hands in her pockets and spelled word after word.

Later, Katharine admitted she was not as cool as she looked. Her hand was in her pocket to hold her good-luck charm. It worked!

2006:
When 13-year-old Katharine Close won the national spelling bee in 2006, it was her fifth time in the finals.

Defender

By Linda Sue Park

Everyone wants to get the ball,
run with it, and score a goal.
But when we win one-nothing,
that "nothing" means everything.

It's tough, playing for nothing.
Defense: Intense immense suspense.

SPELLBOUND

By Sara Holbrook

Confluence

and recompense,

aphid,

ibex,

muse,

chrysalis and zygote.

Words

I know I'll never use.

But like

gossamer and quell,

I had to learn to spell.

Activity Central

YOU'RE A STAR!

When you reach a goal or do something important, you might receive a Certificate of Achievement.

A certificate is a special award that tells what someone has accomplished. Here's an example:

Certificate Title

Person's Name

Activity

Date

CERTIFICATE OF ACHIEVEMENT

Super Speller

This award is presented to

Noah Lane

for winning Mesa Elementary School's

Third-Grade Spelling Bee

On this day of *April 8*   Presented by *Anna Day*

Achievement

Signature

Think about the partner you interviewed last week. Reread your interview notes. Use them to make a Certificate of Achievement for your partner. Then give the certificate to your friend.

60

Become a Character

Many characters in stories achieve goals. Think of a character you've read about who is an achiever. It could be one of the soccer players in the magazine article "A New Team of Heroes," or it could be a character in another story you read this year.

Take a sheet of poster board. Cut a hole for your face.

Decorate the board to look like your character. Go before the class and tell your classmates your story:

▸ who you are
▸ what you achieved
▸ how you achieved it
▸ why you are proud of what you did

Be sure to speak clearly while making eye contact with your classmates.

Extra! Extra!

Read All About Me!

You've been reading about students who are achievers, including soccer players and spellers.

Now it's your turn!

Think about something you've done that you're proud of, or something you've dreamed of doing. Take the role of a reporter and write a newspaper article that tells the world about your accomplishment.

Writing Tips

* Start your article by telling what you accomplished.

* Tell how it happened, and where and when it took place.

* Include a quotation telling how you feel about reaching your goal.

63

Acting Across Generations

EVANSTON, ILLINOIS When the Evanston Children's Theatre decided to put on a play of *Charlotte's Web*, they invited kids from eight to twelve years old to try out for parts. They asked seniors age 55 and older to try out too. Usually, child actors wear gray wigs and paste on fake beards and moustaches to look old. This group uses real seniors.

A few years ago, the Evanston city council decided that the children's theater would have its home in the Levy Center, Evanston's new senior center. So it just seemed natural to get both the kids and the seniors working together.

This experiment has worked well for several plays. Kids play most parts. It's a children's theater group, after all. But seniors have one or two roles in each play.

The Evanston Children's Theatre

The Levy Center holds different senior classes. Seniors who take acting classes try out for the children's theater. Working with kids keeps seniors young. Working with seniors helps kids, too. The seniors share tips from their acting classes, and the kids show what they've learned.

To put on a play, actors must help one another. If a senior forgets some lines, kids jump right in and move the scene along. Seniors do the same for the kids. Once a senior got sick after the first show. A kid took on the senior's part. The show must go on—and it did!

Putting on plays is great fun, but the Evanston Children's Theatre gives seniors and kids a chance to help one another. Bravo!

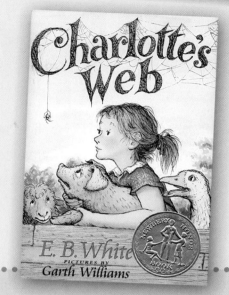

The Evanston Children's Theatre has become very popular. In fact, more than 300 people came to a Sunday afternoon performance of *Charlotte's Web*.

Seniors and children act in a play together.

SAVING BUSTER

"Go get it, boy!" Mrs. Parker yelled as she tossed Buster's favorite ball across the yard. Donovan Lowe was pulling weeds in the Parkers' front yard. He watched Buster streak by and smiled. Donovan liked Mrs. Parker. A year ago she'd had a stroke. That's when she moved in with her daughter Liz, Donovan's neighbor.

The stroke left Mrs. Parker weak enough to need a wheelchair, but it didn't affect her funny bone. Everyone loved her jokes and stories. She was like the whole neighborhood's grandmother. Buster was her service dog, and he was like the whole neighborhood's pet.

He raced back with the ball.

"Okay!" Mrs. Parker laughed. "But this is the last time! I'm exhausted!"

Mrs. Parker threw the ball again. It bounced and rolled into the street. At that exact moment, a truck swung around the corner. There was no way the driver could stop in time.

"*Buuuussss-terrrrr!*" both Donovan and Mrs. Parker shouted.
Donovan sped to the curb where Buster lay. The truck driver was
kneeling beside the dog.

"Get a blanket and call the vet!" he yelled to Donovan. "Tell
them it's an emergency, and we're on our way!"

That night Donovan and his mom brought her tortilla
casserole over to the Parkers. Liz reported what the vet had told
them. "Dr. Sims thinks that Buster will need to go to the animal
hospital in the city for an operation. She'll call tomorrow when she
knows more."

The next morning, Donovan waited nervously for news about
Buster. Around ten o'clock, Liz called. Donovan stayed near until
his mother hung up. "Buster has two broken legs," his mom said.
"The doctors will operate today. You and I will help out with Mrs.
Parker while Liz is at the animal hospital."

Donovan and Mrs. Parker looked at old photo albums while they waited for Liz. They shared funny stories about Buster. Donovan's mom did what she always did in times of stress. She cooked.

Liz returned late that evening. Buster would have casts on his legs for a while, but he'd be all right.

Mrs. Parker and Donovan played a game as his mother heated some food for Liz. Then Donovan went into the kitchen to get a glass of water. Mom and Liz were washing dishes and didn't hear him come in.

"We don't have two thousand dollars to pay for Buster's care!" Liz exclaimed. "I don't know how we'll ever pay it."

Donovan slipped back into the living room. He had $17 he had saved for a new computer game. He'd give it to Liz, but Liz needed two thousand dollars. What else could he do?

That night, Donovan told his mom what he had overheard. "I want to help, but I don't know how."

Mom said softly, "It's a big problem, honey. Sleep on it. Maybe in the morning, we'll have an idea."

No brilliant idea came to Donovan during the night. Nor did one come during school the next day. When he got home, his mom was testing a new recipe. "Taste this, please," she said as she held a spoonful of stew under his nose.

Donovan cleaned the spoon and declared, "Delicious! You should have a cooking show."

"Thank you! I made enough for Liz and Mrs. Parker too. Would you carry it over for me?" Mom asked.

Liz was on the phone as she answered the door. She pointed Donovan to the kitchen. "Just put it anywhere," she whispered as she turned back to her phone conversation.

Donovan stared at the counters. It seemed as if all their neighbors had sent food. Donovan squeezed his bowl in between two dishes. Then he stopped to see how Mrs. Parker was holding up.

"I'm fine, but it's hard on Liz. She has to do everything that Buster used to do for me."

And worry about how she's going to pay the vet bill, Donovan thought.

"What did your mom send over?" Mrs. Parker asked.

"Stew," said Donovan. "But I think you have a wide menu to choose from tonight. I haven't seen that many dishes since the school's potluck supper."

Mrs. Parker whispered, "I know. But your mom's the best cook around."

Donovan smiled. He thought so too. As he walked home, that brilliant idea he'd been waiting for started brewing in his head. As his thoughts sped up, so did his feet.

Donovan burst into the kitchen and announced, "I know how to pay for Buster's operation! We'll have a potluck cooking contest! People can pay to enter. They'll make a sample of food for the judges to taste and a large pot for people to eat. Then people can pay to eat the food!"

The more his mother and Donovan talked, the more excited they became. People could buy tickets for $2 each. Each ticket would pay for a helping from a pot they wanted to taste.

Ideas flowed quickly after that. They'd have cooking contests for adults and for kids. Someone could sell pictures of people and their pets. Others could demonstrate what service dogs do. They could even have a Funniest-Looking Pet contest. They would call it the Pet Potluck Fair. Mrs. Lowe checked with Liz, Mrs. Parker, and some neighbors. Everyone loved their idea.

The day of the potluck contest came. Friends and neighbors filled the park. Buster was the guest of honor. He sat in a special wagon next to Mrs. Parker. Donovan helped sell food tickets. Liz took pictures of people with their pets. Mrs. Parker and Buster judged the pet contest. A bulldog was chosen the funniest-looking pet. It wasn't a surprise when Donovan's mom won the cooking contest. But the best moment came at the end of the day.

Carl Baca was a banker who lived on Donovan's street. He made a special announcement. "Buster has shown us how important a service dog can be. Because we care, we've raised more than one thousand dollars toward Buster's vet bill!" The crowd hollered and clapped.

Donovan hollered and clapped too, but he knew that it wasn't enough. Liz was about to thank the crowd when Mr. Baca held up a hand. "When Donovan Lowe talked to me about raising money for Buster, I made a vow. I told myself that my bank would do all it could to help raise this money. I talked to other businesses in our neighborhood too. And we will make up the difference. We will donate the rest of the money needed to pay Buster's vet bill."

The crowd hollered and clapped even more. Liz laughed and cried at the same time. So did Mrs. Lowe and Mrs. Parker. Buster looked up at Donovan. Donovan could have sworn Buster was smiling. And that was all the thanks Donovan needed.

Company's Coming

David L. Harrison

What a mess!
A total wreck!
They're nearly here!
All hands on deck!

Clear the table!
Grab the shoes!
Make the beds!
No time to lose!

Cram the closets!
Slam the doors!
Hang the jackets!
Mop the floors!

Shove those socks
And underwear
And magazines
Beneath a chair!

Faster! Faster!
Not enough!
Move it! Shake it!
Hide this stuff!

Get some crackers
On a plate!
Pray that they
Are running late!

Slice the cheese!
Put out the cat!
Someone check
That thermostat!

Change the soap
And wipe the tile!
We're all sweaty!

Smile!   Ding Dong!

Discuss Poetry
What patterns of rhymes and beats can you find in this poem? How are lines divided? How do the exclamation points make the poem sound and feel?

You read the story.
Now come see the play!

Charlotte's Web

Charlotte and Wilbur and all their friends on stage!

For three days only
Friday, Saturday, and Sunday
October 12-14
7:00 p.m.

Story Theater
2525 West Main Street

Tickets on sale at the theater now!

This poster does two things: it grabs your attention and gives information.

Make a poster of your own. Think of an event you would want people to come to. It could be a play, a race, a bake sale, or a fun fair. Plan what you will put on your poster and how you will grab people's attention. Then start writing and drawing.

One Plus One ...Equals One!

It's not math, but when it comes to making words, one plus one can equal one. A **compound** word is one word made up of two smaller words.

Example:

grand + mother = grandmother

On another piece of paper, use the picture clues to make a compound word from two small words. The words in the box below are in the compound words you will write. Some words are used twice.

Words Used

boat
drum
pin
chair
ear
stick
dog
house
wheel

1. + = _____?_____

2. + = _____?_____

3. + = _____?_____

4. + = _____?_____

5. + = _____?_____

6. + = _____?_____

The Fair Needs

Often a big problem like Buster's accident takes many people to help solve it. A fair is a fun way to solve a problem. Think of a problem that you would like to help solve by holding a fair. Maybe your school playground needs more equipment. Maybe a local pet shelter needs a bigger building. Write a letter to a newspaper to persuade other people to help you put on a fair. Give reasons that are right for your audience, and use persuasive words. Write with a confident tone.

- Explain the problem.
- Give reasons why people should help.
- Describe the kind of fair you want to hold.
- Tell exactly what your readers can do to help.

YOU!

Credits

Photo Credits

KEY: (t) top, (b) bottom, (l) left, (r) right, (c) center, (bg) background, (fg) foreground, (i) inset

Cover (bg) Bobby Model/National Geographic Society; (cl) Colin Young-Wolff/Photo Edit; (bl) Mike Kemp/Getty Images; RA2 (tl) SSPL via Getty Images; RA3 (tr) PhotoDisc/Getty Images; RA15 (br) Robert E Daemmrich/Getty Images; RA17 (tr) Hulton Archive/Getty Images; (cr) SSPL via Getty Images; RA18 (bl) SSPL via Getty Images; (tl) Time & Life Pictures/Getty Images; RA19 (tc) American Stock/Getty Images; RA19 (cr) Apic/Getty Images; RA20 (bc) John Springer Collection/Corbis; RA21 (tr) Silver Screen Collection/Hulton Archive/Getty Images; RA22 (bl) Luc Roux/Corbis; RA23 (cr) Buyenlarge/Buyenlarge/Time Life Pictures/Getty Images; (br) Close Murray/Corbis SYGMA; RA25 (inset) Louie Psihoyos/Science Faction/Corbis; RA26 (bg) Jupiterimages/Getty Images; RA27 (bg) Jupiterimages/Getty Images; RA28 (br) Tara Moore; RA30 (bc) Adamsmith; RA32 (b) Dennis MacDonald / Alamy; RA33 (inset) Bruce Martin / Alamy; RA34 (cr) Bettmann/Corbis; RA35 (bl) Comstock / Getty Images; (tr) Nick Dolding/cultura/Corbis; RA36 (b) John Giustina; RA38 (bc) Martyn Annetts / Alamy; RA39 (b) blickwinkel / Alamy; RA40 (bg) Fuse ; RA60 (cl) PhotoDisc/Getty Images; (bl) PhotoDisc/Getty Images; RA61 (bc) Open Door/Alamy; (r) PhotoDisc/Getty Images; RA72 (b) Monashee Frantz/Getty Images; Title Page (bg) Didrik Johnck/Corbis; (t) AP Photo/United States Postal Service; 1 (bl) AP Photo/United States Postal Service; (br) F. Lukasseck/Masterfile; (br) AP Photo/United States Postal Service; (bc) AP Photo/United States Postal Service; (tr) Bettmann/Corbis; (tl) Suzanna Price/Getty Images; 2 (bl) Comstock Images/Getty Images; 3 (tr) Alex Wong/Getty Images; 4 (b) F. Lukasseck/Masterfile; (bg) PhotoDisc, Inc./Getty Images; (t) Barbara Strnadova/Photo Researchers, Inc.; (b) Carol Farneti Foster/Getty Images; 6 (l) Bettmann/Corbis; 7 (b) Bettmann/Corbis; 8 (b) Bettmann/Corbis; 10 (b) © James Steinberg / Photo Researchers, Inc.; 11 (t) Underwood & Underwood/Corbis; 12 (br) Tom Strattman/Getty Images; 13 (br) dk/Alamy; (bl) Ilene MacDonald/Alamy; 15 (bg) Dynamic Graphics/Jupiterimages/Getty Images; (bg) Alamy; 16 (all) AP Photo/United States Postal Service; 21 (bl) Suzanna Price/Getty Images; (tr) Colin Young-Wolff/Photo Edit; 22 (bl) sciencephotos/Alamy; (br) sciencephotos/Alamy; (tr) Michal Newman/PhotoEdit; 23 (tr) Hulton-Deutsch Collection/Corbis; (b) © Paul Rapson / Photo Researchers, Inc.; 24 (b) Lester Lefkowitz/Corbis; 25 (br) Hemera/AgeFotostock; (tr) Don Farrall/PhotoDisc/Getty Images; 26 (b) Thomas Michael Corcoran/PhotoEdit; (b) Astra Production/Picture Press/PhotoLibrary; 27 (bl) Matthias Kulka/zefa/Corbis; (c) Corbis; 32 (b) Dennis MacDonald/Alamy; 33 (b) Frank Boxler/AP Images; (t) Brian Kersey/AP Images; 34 Didrik Johnck/Corbis; 36 (bg) PhotoDisc/GettyImages; 37 (cr) altrendo images/Getty Images; (tr) imagebroker/Alamy; 38 (fg) PhotoDisc/GettyImages; (r) Didrik Johnck/Corbis; (l) Gavin Attwood/Touch the Top; 42 (bg) Photodisc, Inc/Getty Images; Comstock Images/Getty Images; 43 (r) Rudi Von Briel/PhotoEdit; 44 (b) image100/Alamy; 46 (b) Michael A. Keller/Corbis; 56 (b) Jeff Hutchens/Getty Images; (t) Alex Wong/Getty Images; 57 (b) Chip Somodevilla/Getty Images; 58 (bg) David Young-Wolff; 59 Digital Vision/Alamy; 64 (b) Bill Nesius; 65 (b) Paul Barton/Corbis; 79 (bl) i love images/Alamy; (cr) Steve Warmowski/The Image Works; (br) Mary Ellen Bartley/Getty Images.

All other photos are property of Houghton Mifflin Harcourt.